Kurt Vonnegut's Crusade

Or,

How a Postmodern Harlequin Preached a New Kind of Humanism

THE SUNY SERIES IN
POSTMODERN CULTURE

Joseph Natoli, *Editor*

Kurt Vonnegut's Crusade

Or,

How a Postmodern Harlequin Preached a New Kind of Humanism

TODD F. DAVIS

State University of New York Press

Published by
State University of New York Press, Albany

© 2006 State University of New York

All rights reserved

Printed in the United States of America

For information, address State University of New York Press, 194 Washington Avenue, Suite 305, Albany, NY 12210-2384

Production by Marilyn P. Semerad
Marketing by Anne M. Valentine

Library of Congress Cataloging-in-Publication Data

Davis, Todd F., 1965–
Kurt Vonnegut's crusade; or, How a postmodern harlequin preached a new kind of humanism / Todd F. Davis.
    p. cm. — (SUNY series in postmodern culture)
Includes bibliographical references and index.
ISBN 0-7914-6675-2 (alk. paper)
    1. Vonnegut, Kurt—Criticism and interpretation. 2. Science fiction, American—History and criticism. 3. Postmodernism (Literature)—United States. 4. Humanism in literature. I. Title: Kurt Vonnegut's crusade. II. Title: How a postmodern harlequin preached a new kind of humanism. III. Title. IV. Series.

PS3572.O5Z65 2006
813'.54—dc22

                                                                2005008724
ISBN-13: 978-0-7914-6675-9 (hardcopy : alk. paper)

10 9 8 7 6 5 4 3 2 1

For Kenneth Womack
and James Mellard,
who still believe stories
might change the way we live.

Contents

Acknowledgments

I owe special debts of gratitude to the many friends and colleagues who helped make this volume possible. I am particularly grateful for the encouragement and advice of David Anderson, Ervin Beck, Beth Martin Birky, Harold and Joyce Davis, Shelly, Noah, and Nathan Davis, James Decker, Keith and Tammy Fynaardt, Jim Gorman, Ann Hostetler, Jerome Klinkowitz, Don and Melinda Lanham, David and Vicki Malone, James Mellard, Glenn Meeter, Dinty Moore, Ray and Laurie Peterson, Mary Sue Schriber, Ned Watts, and Kenneth Womack. A special thanks to Kurt Vonnegut for his kindness, his humor, and for the illustration that graces this book's cover and title pages. An additional note of thanks to Joe Petro of Origami Express and the www.vonnegut.com <http://www. vonnegut.com/> website.

1

Postmodern (Midwestern) Morality

The Act of Affirming Humanity in a Screwed-up World

"Hello, babies. Welcome to Earth. It's hot in the summer and cold in the winter. It's round and wet and crowded. At the outside, babies, you've got about a hundred years here. There's only one rule that I know of, babies—:
"God damn it, you've got to be kind."
—Kurt Vonnegut,
God Bless You, Mr. Rosewater

Kurt Vonnegut's Social Commitment: Acting Humane Even When the Odds Are against You

W̲HILE K̲URT V̲ONNEGUT'S reputation as a major American writer has been the subject of much debate for the past thirty years, his status with his readers has remained exceedingly healthy.[1] Vonnegut's devoted reading public, those who have—as Wayne Booth suggests about author–reader relationships in *The Company We*

1

Keep: An Ethics of Fiction—invited the author into their lives,
embracing the negotiated philosophy of a postmodern, Midwestern moralist, have remained faithful in a manner that is humorously akin to the rock-and-roll groupies who followed the Grateful Dead across the country for so many years, or, perhaps even
more so, the citizens of some Indiana town where folks gather
around one of their own boys who's made good, waiting to hear
what he has to say. It is this faithful following—one created by
narratives that are at once profound and intimately familiar, one
which was responsible for the early paperback sales of such works
as *Mother Night* and *Cat's Cradle*—that scholars at first briefly
acknowledged, then ignored. This cult of readers was first mentioned by early critics like John Somer and Jerome Klinkowitz, but
since Vonnegut's commercial success, little has been said about
these readers and their significant influence as they continue to
purchase Vonnegut's work, passing it on to subsequent generations and keeping his entire canon in print—an impressive list of
more than twenty books that Dell has continued to refurbish and
hawk with new cover designs.

My first experience with this group of readers occurred on a
rainy and unseasonably cold evening in November 1991 in the
heart of the country, in the heart of the Midwest. My wife and I,
along with several thousand admirers of Vonnegut, had paid
$12.00 a ticket to listen to the author deliver a speech in the gym-
nasium of William Rainey Harper College just outside of Chicago
in Palatine, Illinois. Vonnegut spoke for an hour and a half, using
portions of articles and speeches that had been collected previously in *Palm Sunday*, as well as more timely material that spoke
directly to political and cultural events from recent weeks (some
of this material subsequently was collected and published in *Fates
Worse Than Death*). Just as in his writing, Vonnegut's mannerisms
and speaking voice helped create an environment of intimacy, of
familiarity. Such an environment may strike some as odd, considering that many critics have labeled Vonnegut an indifferent
philosopher of existentialism or a playful nihilist of comic futility,
but it was quite obvious that the Kurt Vonnegut who spoke compassionately and directly about such issues as violence and war,
love and respect, was exactly the Kurt Vonnegut that the audience
had come to see. Here was the Midwestern sage at the town meeting speaking his mind; here was the town fool making the young
laugh and the old-timers shake their heads. Here was a man who

took seriously the values he learned in his American Civics class at Shortridge High School and was holding his compatriots to those very values—as idealistic as they might be. Yet there was something different about this Midwesterner, something slightly out of kilter, something decidedly postmodern. For that reason, the speaking engagement, at times, more closely resembled a rock concert or political convention than a lecture given by a man of arts and letters. Several times throughout the evening, members of the audience shouted out encouragement or requests for the author to address certain topics, and, at all times, the crowd was attentive, laughing heartily at Vonnegut's pointed barbs that, for the most part, were directed at current political leaders and at all of humanity's ineffectuality in dealing with its daily enigmatic existence. It was clear that these readers—although entertained by narrative structures first developed by Vonnegut in his novels and more often than not punctuated by a joke—had come seeking guidance and understanding—or reassurance—on some very weighty philosophical issues in the wake of the Gulf War.

This sort of environment—one which in tone seemed more familial than scholarly, as members of the audience talked freely to one another concerning characters from the novels and even of Vonnegut himself as if they were old friends or relations—is, of course, the very kind of cultural setting that Vonnegut most believes in. In his books and lectures, Vonnegut consistently preaches about his experience growing up in Indianapolis and the relationship of this Midwestern experience to the theories of Dr. Robert Redfield, whose work Vonnegut was introduced to while studying anthropology at the University of Chicago. Redfield's theories contend that all human beings need to belong to extended families for physical and emotional well-being. But such communities have rapidly disappeared during the modern era, and in the fragmented and disrupted postmodern world are, for the most part, absent. As Vonnegut remarks, "It is curious that such communities should be so rare, since human beings are genetically such gregarious creatures. They need plenty of like-minded friends and relatives almost as much as they need B-complex vitamins and a heartfelt moral code" (*Palm Sunday* 204). Vonnegut, in his speaking and writing, has undoubtedly made progress toward the creation of these kinds of communities, and while this is a result he might not have foreseen, I suspect it is one with which he is quite happy.

Unlike other postmodern writers, like John Barth or Thomas Pynchon in whose company he is often placed, Vonnegut speaks openly about his commitment and responsibility to his readers. This commitment is inextricably bound with Vonnegut's view of literature, the work it may do. Although his stance remains unpopular in many scholarly and artistic circles (and understandably so, considering that it is a position similar to that taken by certain groups who wish to censor the arts), Vonnegut adamantly asserts that artists are agents of change, agents with the ability to do good or harm. As he explains in an interview with *Playboy* later collected in *Conversations with Kurt Vonnegut*, "My motives are political. I agree with Stalin and Hitler and Mussolini that the writer should serve his society. I differ with dictators as to how writers should serve. Mainly, I think they should be—and biologically have to be—agents of change. For the better, we hope" (57).[2]

In *Vonnegut in America*, Klinkowitz suggests that this sense of responsibility results from Vonnegut's early forays into journalism as a writer for student newspapers, first at Shortridge High School in Indianapolis and later at Cornell University (22). During his tenure as a writer for school periodicals, Vonnegut displayed great concern with the political and social issues of the day, with scientific progress heralded as the saving grace of the United States. Issues of scientific progress, of social commitment, of history's absurdly romantic relationship with war would continue to occupy Vonnegut not only in his writing but also in his study: Vonnegut majored in chemistry and biology at Cornell, and later at the University of Chicago pursued a master's degree in anthropology. For Vonnegut, issues of such significance demand that the writer be understood; the goal of the writer is to communicate as quickly and effectively—and quite often for Vonnegut, as ironically and humorously—as possible.[3] While much of Vonnegut's writing maintains standards first established by his work as a student journalist and public relations writer for General Electric, these same standards that have helped him achieve a level of clarity that is seldom encountered in postmodern fiction have been attacked as simplistic by certain adversarial critics.

Roger Sale, in the *New York Times Book Review*, has berated Vonnegut's work (in this case, specifically *Slapstick*) by saying that "Nothing could be easier," while works by Thomas Pynchon take "stamina, determination, and crazy intelligence" (3). Although Vonnegut has had to weather this kind of criticism, he has not stood alone. John Irving, among other writers, defends Vonnegut's craft, pointing to the sheer lunacy of asserting that "what is easy to read has been easy to write" (41). Irving claims that "Vonnegut's lucidity is hard and brave work in a literary world where pure messiness is frequently thought to be a sign of some essential wrestling with the 'hard questions'" (42). Undoubtedly, Vonnegut is wrestling with the "hard questions," and his ability to do so with grace and precision marks him not only as a fine literary stylist but also reveals his ultimate concern: that his ideas find their way to the reader. Vonnegut's own response to literary critics, included in *Palm Sunday*, takes the form of an understated diatribe: "It has been my experience with literary critics and academics in this country that clarity looks a lot like laziness and ignorance and childishness and cheapness to them. Any idea which can be grasped immediately is for them, by definition, something they knew all the time. So it is with literary experimentation, too. If a literary experiment works like a dream, is easy to read and enjoy, the experimenter is a hack" (320).

Whether one agrees that Vonnegut's work is aesthetically pleasing because of its directness, however, is not at issue here. Rather, his desire to enact change, to establish patterns for humanity that will lead to the construction of better realities for the world, will be the focus of this study.[4] As Vonnegut has explained, "I've worried some about why write books when Presidents and Senators and generals do not read them, and the university experience taught me a very good reason: you catch people before they become generals and Senators and Presidents, and you poison their minds with humanity. Encourage them to make a better world" (Allen, *Conversations* 5).

It is Vonnegut's insistence that writing is an "act of good citizenship or an attempt, at any rate, to be a good citizen" (Allen, *Conversations* 72) that has led many critics to dismiss his work. Critics like Peter Prescott denounce Vonnegut for what Prescott calls "gratuitous digressions"; he characterizes Vonnegut's writing on race and pollution and poverty as "arrested," and the relationship of author to audience as "sucking up to kiddy grievances" (40). Prescott is outraged—or as he puts it in a review of *Breakfast of Champions*, "From time to time, it's nice to have a book you can hate—it clears the pipes—and I hate this book for its preciousness" (40)—I argue, for the simple reason that Vonnegut resists the rhetoric of modernist art. By Prescott's modernist standards, a book like *Breakfast of Champions* is "manure, of course." Raymond Olderman argues that Vonnegut's work should be assessed by different criteria: "If we grant that he has designs on us and that he sometimes sacrifices fictive device for absolute clarity, often sounding more like a social scientist than a novelist, then we can forget his occasional failure to justify the literary tradition he half evokes, and judge him on the genuine quality of a passionately honest heart and mind working over the bewildering facts of contemporary existence" (192). While I agree with Olderman that any evaluation of Vonnegut by modernist, new critical standards is certain to find aspects of his work lacking, I do not agree that Vonnegut's only contribution to American literature is a "passionately honest heart and mind working over the bewildering facts of contemporary existence." The very nature of Olderman's defense—one that attempts to excuse Vonnegut for sounding more like a social scientist than a novelist—is situated in modernist thought, using generic paradigms developed by the New Critics, among others.

The new fiction of our times, often labeled postmodern, may, as James M. Mellard suggests, be perceived as an exploded form. In some instances, notions of generic distinction have all but vanished. The writing of Richard Brautigan, William S. Burroughs, Vonnegut, and many others problematized the use of such descriptors and boundaries and helped literary theory to move beyond the work of genre-labeling into new territory. I argue that Vonnegut offers a new kind of fiction, a paradigm of postmodernity that allows the author to struggle with philosophical ideas concerning our condition in a form that reflects this very struggle. Unlike Auden's claim that "poetry makes nothing happen" and the assertion of so many modernist critics that art is autonomous (art for art's sake), Vonnegut is concerned not only with the form his writing takes—one that reflects postmodern convictions about the nature of reality and our ability to express that reality in language—but also with the positive work his artistry may engender. As Jane Tompkins explains in *Sensational Designs: The Cultural Work of American Fiction, 1790–1860*, the novels of writers like Harriet Beecher Stowe were dismissed by modernist academics because such critics failed to acknowledge the kind of "cultural work" that Stowe hoped to bring about with her writing. Sadly, Vonnegut also has received the same treatment at times, neglected by critics and scholars alike because of his social vision, which he claims grew out of his Midwestern upbringing. "That's the story of my life, too. I went to a good high school, and everything was noise after that," Vonnegut remarks in *Like Shaking Hands with God: A Conversation about Writing*. "I was always interested in good citizenship," he continues. "It was just what I learned in junior civics class in school in Indianapolis, how important it is to be a good citizen" (70).

Vonnegut's efforts to connect with his audience as an act of good citizenship, a connection he hopes ultimately leads to the construction of better realities for humanity, are rooted in the "big" questions. His work is philosophical in nature; his stories often take the form of parables; he struggles along with the reader, not in a position of author as omniscient creator but as one who also is wrestling honestly with the "big" question at hand. Arguably, Vonnegut's appeal to college students since their discovery of his work in the 1960s and 1970s may be linked with his ability to explore philosophically profound questions in prose that is neither convoluted nor simply theoretical. Vonnegut explains his popularity with young people as the result of his insistence on probing the nature of our existence: "Maybe it's because I deal with sophomoric questions that full adults regard as settled. I talk about what is God like, what could He want, is there a heaven, and, if there is, what would it be like? This is what college sophomores are into" (Allen, *Conversations* 103).[5] What distinguishes Vonnegut from other metaphysicians is his incredulity toward final answers and his unflagging determination to find pragmatic responses to profound questions. His admonitions to readers, based on the firm conviction that there are no longer "enormous new truths" to be discovered, are mired in what Vonnegut calls "the ordinariness of life, the familiarity of love" (Allen, *Conversations* 74).

While Vonnegut is willing to contemplate the existence of God, of His hand in the painfulness of life for some and the sweetness of life for others, he is not willing to allow theoretical debates to overshadow our need for action in our attempts to alleviate the suffering of others.[6] The working-class pragmatism he inherited from the preceding generations of Vonneguts who lived in Indianapolis—among his ancestors were the proprietors of a long-running hardware store and the architects and builders of many buildings that still dot this Midwestern city's skyline—will not allow Vonnegut to simply theorize. While intellectual inquiry and philosophizing may be important, it will not directly feed those who do not have food or put a roof above the heads of those who sleep in the street. This split between intellectual theorizing and the pragmatic social consequences of such intellectual activity in the physical world, a split that is often not handled by scientists and political leaders to Vonnegut's satisfaction, may have contributed to his attempted suicide in 1984. As he describes it in *Fates Worse Than Death*, "I was carted off to the Emergency Room of St. Vincent's Hospital in the middle of the night to be pumped out. I had tried to kill myself. It wasn't a cry for help. It wasn't a nervous breakdown. . . . I wanted out of here" (181).[7] This revelation, in *Fates Worse Than Death*, follows directly on the heels of a chapter devoted to Vonnegut's trip to Mozambique, where he witnessed the deaths by starvation of little girls about the age of his own daughter Lily, as well as a recollection of a trip he took to Biafra, a small republic in Africa that surrendered unconditionally to Nigeria on 17 January 1970, where he watched in horror as children were denied proper food because of a war blockade, and, as a result, they "all had red hair and their rectums were everted, dangling outside like radiator hoses" (174–75). Put quite simply in the ensuing chapter, Vonnegut explains that he had been "too pissed off to live another minute (absolutely apeshit)" (183).[8]

It is this kind of social awareness that produces such strong convictions in Vonnegut's prose, that allows him to urge others not to see their work in terms of mere word play or philosophical theorizing, that sounds his clarion call for each of us to examine our lives and to live in such a way that we minimize the harm we do to the earth or its inhabitants. Vonnegut is unwilling to accept a discussion of the situation in Mozambique or Biafra or wherever people suffer physically and emotionally that concentrates on the complexity of the political situation or the impossibility of raising financial support to bring supplies to the victims. By this, I do not mean to imply that Vonnegut does not recognize the nuances and labyrinthine nature of wars and poverty and racism. He, in fact, writes a great deal about the difficulty of determining who is a victim and who is an attacker, and, in typical Vonnegut fashion, we are told that seldom can such questions ever be answered. He does, however, conclude that conditions of daily life like those in Mozambique are "no more to be discussed in terms of good and evil than cholera, say, or bubonic plague" (*Fates* 169). In Vonnegut's mind, the physical needs of people can never be evaluated in terms of good and evil. No esoteric or theoretical debate, according to Vonnegut, should impinge upon our response to cholera or bubonic plague or starvation. Vonnegut is our leading literary pragmatist. Although he enjoys thinking through—or, at the very least, pondering with great energy and humor—the problems of our existence, including the politics of nations and the practices of religions, he ultimately is concerned with the physical and emotional care of humanity: the weak and downtrodden, first, and those more fortunate, second.

While Vonnegut has a deep respect for science and philosophy—he often proudly recites the accomplishments of his brother, Bernard, who graduated with a doctorate from MIT and was a highly respected scientist responsible for such discoveries as the effect of silver iodide in the artificial creation of rain or snow—at no time is he willing to place the study of either science or philosophy above the practical concerns of everyday life. It is human life, its dignity, that Vonnegut wishes most to preserve. In an address at MIT in 1985, Vonnegut warned future scientists of the danger in perceiving their intellectual pursuits as neutral.[9] He illustrated this point with examples from history; perhaps the most horrific and tragic example concerns Hitler's hope to eradicate from Germany all Jews, Gypsies, Slavs, homosexuals, and Communists, a hope that might never have been accomplished except for the help of chemists who supplied Hitler's executioners with cyanide gas.[10] Vonnegut's conclusion: "It can make quite a difference not just to you but to humanity: the sort of boss you choose, whose dreams you help come true" (*Fates* 118).

Some might criticize Vonnegut for such a facile statement. This way of thinking, however, actually fits quite comfortably with the philosophical thought of our age. Vonnegut, like other postmodernists, believes that claims for objectivity and neutrality no longer hold water; rather, he acknowledges that observations and inventions and actions of all sorts are subjective in nature, carrying ethical and political implications. Therefore, Vonnegut's conclusion, although seemingly naive, is couched in the discourse of postmodernity that believes it has exposed as a charade the modernist pretense to objectivity and neutrality, and, fittingly, he ends his speech by imploring the students of MIT to rewrite the Hippocratic Oath in order that it might apply to all scientists, "remembering that all sciences have their roots in the simple wish to make people safe and well" (*Fates* 120). Vonnegut suggests the oath begin like this: "The regimen I adopt shall be for the benefit of all life on this planet, according to my own ability and judgment, and not for its hurt or for any wrong. I will create no deadly substance or device, though it be asked of me, nor will I counsel such" (*Fates* 120). Surely this kind of rhetoric would describe quite nicely the unwritten oath of Vonnegut's own work, the work of a postmodern moralist whose roots reach back to his youth in Indianapolis.

If I am, however, to represent the range of Vonnegut's philosophy, I cannot ignore what is often misconstrued as his devotion to a dark nihilism that impedes his morality or ethical position. Charles B. Harris, in an essay entitled "Illusion and Absurdity: The Novels of Kurt Vonnegut," contends that "Vonnegut's belief in a purposeless universe constitutes his main theme" (131), that his books, at all times, comment upon the "futility of human endeavor, the meaninglessness of human existence" (133). Harris's remarks are representative of a branch of Vonnegut studies that emphasizes the note of despondency, the hopelessness on which so many of the early novels end. While Harris's claim that Vonnegut's work fits nicely with absurdist philosophy seems plausible, he ignores the ethical frame that Vonnegut develops in conjunction with this philosophy. Like many of the French absurdists, who actively worked for political and social improvement, Vonnegut also wishes to create and promote an ethic that ennobles humanity. Unlike Harris, I contend that Vonnegut's ethical position constitutes his main theme, that he is more concerned with our response to existence than with the philosophical nature of that existence. Certainly novels like *Cat's Cradle*, with its understated apocalyptic conclusion thumbing its nose at God, and *Sirens of Titan*, with its absurd punch line explaining humanity's triumphs and sufferings as an elaborate tool for the Tralfamadorian messages concerning a repair part for a stranded spacecraft, suggest a purposeless universe, but that does not necessarily mean our grappling with futility is meaningless. Upon closer examination, what we find in Vonnegut's work is an appraisal of our current condition on the planet that leads him to conclude that the universe is indeed absurd.

Yet Vonnegut does not succumb to the darkness. His writing is prophetic; his stories of a bleak future prompt the reader to look at the current condition of the planet and its inhabitants while

offering an ethical position that gives meaning to human life. Vonnegut's belief that the universe is purposeless is not his main
theme; it is his assumption. Vonnegut's main theme remains his
call to common decency and his hope that we will learn to respect
one another before we destroy ourselves and the planet. Therefore, in each novel, despite the sometimes disheartening sense of
futility that pervades it, Vonnegut does offer suggestions for better living and hope for the despondent. In *Cat's Cradle*, Vonnegut
actually works out the ideas of Robert Redfield in a fictional setting. This novel, which served as Vonnegut's master's thesis in
anthropology, explores the very real physical and emotional needs
of humans, needs that he claims may be met by the value structures found in folk societies. The positive example of religion
offered by Vonnegut in *Cat's Cradle*, a religion called Bokononism
and based on foma (or harmless untruths), exhibits characteristics
similar to folk societies and proposes that religion—an institution
that Vonnegut, while criticizing its historical practice, consistently
praises for its potential to satisfy the needs of humans—may be
founded on a floating center that acknowledges its own fallibility,
its own constructedness, and the never-ending possibilities of life.[11]
Bokononism differs from other established religions in its reluctance to claim an absolutist position; it is based on *The Books of
Bokonon*, a religious text that is forever changing, expanding:
"There is no such thing as a completed copy" (*Cat's* 124). It is,
finally, the religion of science that drives the novel to its dark conclusion. Bokononism, the hopeful act of social protest at the center of the novel, is not ultimately responsible for the end of the
world. Rather, the naiveté of science—its belief that the pursuit of
scientific "truth" is neutral—establishes a space in which ice-nine,
a substance more deadly in its consequence than any number of
atomic bombs, may be created and then distributed to the family
of its creator. Predictably, the different emotional needs of the
family members, needs that their father, the man of science, could
not satisfy, prevail, and the "pure" substance of ice-nine falls into
the hands of those who do not care to see the world go on spin-
ning. Although *Cat's Cradle* ends tragically, to claim that Vonnegut subscribes to a fatalistic view of the human condition, that
he believes existence is meaningless, is to ignore a plethora of evidence to the contrary.[12] Similarly, in *Sirens of Titan*, although
Malachi Constant discovers that human history is actually the
story of the Tralfamadorian attempt to deliver a mechanical part

to Salo for the repair of his spacecraft, the "moral" of the story—
a "moral" closely related to Eliot Rosewater's pronouncement to
Mary Moody's twins: "God damn it, you've got to be kind" (*God
Bless* 110)—seems to be embedded in Malachi's belated revelation
of the purpose of human existence: "It took us that long to realize that a purpose of human life, no matter who is controlling it,
is to love whoever is around to be loved" (313).

It is true that Vonnegut often depicts the plight of humanity in
brutally honest terms: He is unwilling to wear rose-colored glasses
in order to pander to those who wish only to hear euphemistic
sound bites about our future. As he sees it, the uncontained
growth of population, the destructive and costly wars that enliven
an economic machine that uses human flesh for fuel, our blithe
response to the devastation of the environment, and our continued
mistreatment of one another, does not bode well for the future.
Vonnegut, however, does not see himself as fatalistic or pessimistic; as he explains, "When I'm engaged in any action I have
to take into consideration that many of the people on either side
of me don't care what happens next. I am mistrustful of most people as custodians of life and so I'm pessimistic on that account. I
think that there are not many people who want life to go on. And
I'm just a bearer of bad tidings really" (Allen, *Conversations* 233).
Vonnegut's view of his own writing then may be construed as
journalistic; he is reporting on the condition of the world and the
failure of our current response to it; he is not advocating this
response. Vonnegut, in a characteristically macabre one-liner,
offers this epitaph for the Earth: "We could have saved it, but we
were too darn cheap and lazy" (*Fates* 185). This bleak portrayal
of the current situation does not preclude hope or necessitate
despair on Vonnegut's part. As indicated by the first clause in the
above quotation, we do have the ability to save our planet, to
make life better; it is our insistence that all is well or, at the other
end of the spectrum, our self-loathing and despair that too often
leads to inaction and an acceptance of the status quo.

Vonnegut's career ought to be seen in terms of a fight against
our inaction and our blunders that too often harm us, as well as the
planet. Undoubtedly, there is a dark vein of ideas and images that
run through the work of Vonnegut, and this vein, which he shares
with the writer he most admires, Mark Twain, encourages some
critics to characterize his work as despairingly nihilistic.[13] Yet Vonnegut's response to existence seems anything but despairing. In fact,

his determination to write toward some kind of action that might shift our paths toward something better, something worth giving to future generations, leads him to say, "I find that I trust my own writing most, and others seem to trust it most, too, when I sound most like a person from Indianapolis, which is what I am" (*Palm Sunday* 77). As a person from Indianapolis who was reared on the idealistic notions of freedom and liberty and justice for all peoples, Vonnegut's use of fiction becomes activist in nature; it is his hope that he may shock his readers into a moment of comprehension, a moment in which they may recognize the irrationality of our political or religious practices, our industrial or legal abuses, and move on toward a world that follows more closely the ideals of his youth.

Vonnegut moves beyond the recognition of our current condition as shockingly futile and begins to make attempts at alleviating the painful oppression of those circumstances that create the very futility he chronicles by composing fictions that serve as a mirror to our condition. Moreover, Vonnegut's movement toward action through the writing of fiction appears to transcend the modernist paradigm, recognizing the pluralist nature of reality and the postmodern deconstruction of metanarratives. The petites histoires—small localized narratives for living—that Vonnegut offers are based on traditional humanist values but do not operate within a grand narrative or a totalizing schema as such narratives once did. For Vonnegut, there is never a dogmatic claim to "truth." As a writer, he refuses totalizing structures and consistently reminds the reader of the constructedness of reality, of the textuality in the texts that he himself has written, of the limitations involved in his prescriptive postmodern morality. The postmodern move toward an understanding of the development of metanarratives and how such metanarratives have been used in the past to justify atrocities committed by Western culture brings to bear the issues of essence and value. Some postmodernists have abandoned any notion of the actual existence of essence or value, and, as a result, they have been criticized as immoral or amoral. Perhaps the most significant contribution Vonnegut has made is his example of postmodern activism in his writing and in his life outside writing, an activism that intersects repeatedly with powerful social concern and commitment to local and global conflicts. Vonnegut's social vision, rooted in a provisional morality and a pattern of local, relational, and contextual value, refuses to ignore the emotional and physical suffering of any creature.

Postmodern Possibilities

To define postmodernism is a harrowing project. In fact, the very act of defining seems to fly in the face of postmodernity: can there be any single, essential definition of postmodernism? If one accepts the theoretical principles of poststructuralist thought, the answer must be a resounding no. Interestingly enough, this contradiction certainly has not reduced the number of texts attempting to establish a static definition of postmodernism and produced by an academic industry that Fredric Jameson would undoubtedly see as an effect of late capitalism. What I propose, then, is to situate this study amidst the cacophony of competing voices, creating a context in which we may understand in what ways Vonnegut is postmodern. What postmodernism "means" cannot be found in unified or totalizing explanations. Rather, there are myriad postmodernisms: some describing postmodernity as a historical epoch; some focusing on the visual arts since World War II; some concentrating on the literary innovations of writers like Barth and Pynchon and Vonnegut. There is no consensus about postmodernity, only endless multiplicities. To acknowledge the pluralistic nature of postmodern discourse and to recognize that any one definition of the many possible definitions may only work at the local level within, in this case, the context of an academic community is to embrace the theoretical project of postmodernity: work is at all times relational. Therefore, although it is clear that much of the writing that has been done over the last forty years is quite different from that of the previous generation, any effort to form a static postmodern poetics must always remain just that: an effort, a gesture.

Perhaps John McGowan offers the most concise and least exclusive definition of postmodernism: "At the very least, postmodernism highlights the multiplication of voices, questions, and conflicts that has shattered what once seemed to be (although it never really was) the placid unanimity of the great tradition and of the West that gloried in it" ("Postmodernism" 587). A most significant feature of postmodernism revolves around its continued deconstruction of any unified or unifying image: the "reality" of postmodernity lies in its awareness of the constructed nature of "truth" and the ensuing efforts to allow voices, once silenced by the modern monomyth of one essential "truth," to speak from the margins. Not surprisingly, Vonnegut has embraced this notion of relative truth and speaks strongly about the need for education to introduce the voices of other cultures: "I didn't learn until I was in college about all the other cultures, and I should have learned that in the first grade. A first-grader should understand that his culture isn't a rational invention; that there are thousands of other cultures and they all work pretty well; that all cultures function on faith rather than truth; that there are lots of alternatives to our own society" (Allen, *Conversations* 104).

Following the example of many other theorists, perhaps the most effective manner in which to approach a definition of postmodernism is to place it in relation to our understanding of modernism.[14] Because of Vonnegut's own interest in science and anthropology, it is fitting to begin by examining the dynamic changes in scientific study, changes that first affected the nature of investigation in biology, chemistry, and physics and later changed the way in which we view art and culture. James B. Miller argues that the prevailing images for the premodern world were organic while those for the modern world were mechanical and dualistic; he asserts that in the postmodern world the representative images are historical, relational, and personal (8). To be sure, the works of Darwin and other evolutionary theorists contributed to the shift from organicism to mechanism, and even though postmodernity uses certain evolutionary concepts, further suggesting the influence of Darwinian theory, their application is markedly different. While the modern perspective of science held that there was "objective knowledge which derives from detached, impersonal observation of the facts of nature," the postmodern perspective suggests that no amount or quality of observation can offer a full and complete description: "It suggests that at the core of reality is an unfathomable mystery" (James Miller 10).

Although we may in part understand evolution, we cannot apprehend what an entity may become or entirely understand what it has been. Moreover, judging by contemporary attempts to discern the state of our present development, the act of describing a species' current evolutionary condition would seem even more tenuous. The world is at all times in process; it is not a creation so much as a *creating* (James Miller 9). In addition to the influence of evolutionary theory, the development of Einstein's Theory of Relativity undermines the modern and premodern concept of essence. Existence is at all times relational; we cannot understand any part of life without first perceiving its participatory nature.

We no longer live in a Newtonian world in which absolute con-
texts were thought to exist. Moreover, quantum theory overturns
any notion of a universe comprised of self-sufficient things; Miller
contends that in the postmodern world "the universe does not
seem to be composed of stuff or things at all but rather of dynamic
relations" (9). These advances in scientific theory—advances that
work naturally into Vonnegut's own writing as a result of his
undergraduate and graduate study and later professional interests—continue to disrupt and subvert not only the practices of
biology, chemistry, and physics but also the traditionally humanist disciplines of literature and art. These significant and radical
disruptions in scientific thought and the technology that has
resulted from such advances have created an environment in
which it is hard to imagine a reality or essence that might be com-
prehended outside of some context. With the information superhighway, ushered in by computer technology (the internet and e-
mail, for example), satellite communications, and the seemingly
endless number of channels offered on demand by contemporary
television programming, an entire generation looks to a future
where knowing what is happening in a neighborhood in Kenya or
Iraq or Sri Lanka and knowing what is happening in one's own
neighborhood in Boston or San Francisco are commensurate. No
longer can cultures be dismissed easily by a single set of criteria
issued forth by some dominant Western ideology; the technological advances of postmodernity help establish a space for groups of
people who once were exploited or, worse, destroyed, to assert the
validity of local knowledge over universal knowledge.

    Because of the amazing and, at times, frightening dispersal of
information, contemporary generations may have difficulty imag-
ining how there could have ever been a time where a small number of metanarratives controlled the ways a nation thought and
talked about such issues as foreign policy or justice. When I speak
of a time in history where as a culture we showed allegiance to
several grand narratives, I do not mean to imply that all people
responded in a like manner to these narratives because, of course,
those at the margins who did not fit into the "truth" of certain
grand narratives remained on the periphery, isolated by their "oth-
erness." It also should be noted that grand narratives continue to
function in our culture today. Certainly since the tragedy of 9/11
and the ensuing war on terror we have witnessed a revival or a
return to a reliance on a more monolithic narrative of American

righteousness and patriotism. In addition, while our culture continues to diversify into multiplicities, we still are controlled by what Jameson calls late capitalism. Our financial structures, the very ways we create commerce, are based on a particular grand narrative, and critics like Jameson who are frightened to think where our commodification of indigenous cultures, the generic exploitation of those very multiplicities we work hard to validate, will lead us, rally against some of the practices of postmodernism. These criticisms of the exploitation of local custom and knowledge watered down and packaged only to be fed to a consumer culture are more than fair, and we would be wise to heed such prophetic warnings. Although the information superhighway contributes positively to the characteristically postmodern move toward multiplicity and relativity, it should be noted that there are inherent dangers in what kinds of information may be disseminated, a problem we will return to later.

Jean-François Lyotard claims that the postmodern condition is a result of "the crisis of narratives" (xiii). In *The Postmodern Condition: A Report on Knowledge*, Lyotard explains that scholarly activity in the modern world may be defined as "any science that legitimates itself with reference to a metadiscourse . . . making an explicit appeal to some grand narrative" (71–72). He briefly defines the postmodern as an "incredulity toward metanarratives" (72). Postmodernity refuses the authority of modern metanarratives, attacking their discourse on the grounds that they are logocentric, linear, and totalizing; such narratives claim to be scientific and objective while reaffirming modernity and its truth. The truth of modernity, of course, excludes most of the world, establishing as normative Western European and American ideas/ideals. Postmodernists argue against such metanarratives, claiming that reason, objectivity, and essential truth are merely effects of discourse. Pauline Marie Rosenau explains in *Postmodernism and the Social Sciences: Insights, Inroads, and Intrusions* that postmodernity sees truth claims as merely the "product of power games, manipulated into position by those whose interests they serve" (78). As this study hopes to suggest through readings of Vonnegut's individual novels, the exposure of modern metanarratives and the subsequent deconstruction of the illusory but controlling discourse that helps to propagate their myths of essential truth remain a consistent target for Vonnegut throughout his career.

But where may we go after the deconstruction of grand narratives? How does a culture that has heretofore based its systems of socialization—its institutions of government, legislation, and religion—on the ideas of essence and value, ideas that have been shown quite convincingly to be effects of discourse, move into an era of multiplicity, of plurality, of "truths" not "truth"? Certainly this bold step into the postmodern frightens and unnerves many while disturbing others to such a degree that they fight even the smallest deviation from modernist presuppositions with tenacity and vitriol. One possible reason for the anxious resistance of some to postmodern ideas hinges on the nebulous position of those very theorists who boldly entered the fray, tearing apart the facade of modernism brick by brick with no clear notion of what would be rebuilt, if anything could be rebuilt. Many theorists who savagely destroyed the oppressive myths of the past were surprised to find that their own work, when scrutinized by Derridian principles, also fell into similar aporetic states; it soon became clear that all discourse harbors bias, that there is no place where one can speak neutrally or innocently. In the postmodern world, there is no position of universality from which to theorize; there can only be local philosophizing leading to micro-theory, and, paradoxically, postmodern theorists must admit that a position that insists upon the deconstruction of metanarratives and the singular possibility of small, locally based narratives is itself a totalizing position, perhaps the only metanarrative to which postmodernity subscribes. The space opened by these critics, however, should not be devalued; certainly the positive political action that results from this work, leading to the formation of new discourses like feminism and multiculturalism, owes much to the ideas posited by earlier postmodern theorists. The contemporary assimilation and revaluation of the position of women and other minorities, the new turn toward indigenous cultures that infiltrates such diverse areas of our society as educational curriculum reviews from kindergarten through graduate school and corporate marketing strategies at the local, national, and international level, undoubtedly would never have appeared with such force and rapidity without the positive work of postmodern theory. If postmodernity is, in part, responsible for exposing the rhetorical nature of truth and value, two linguistic structures that have been appealed to in order to justify such heinous acts as the destruction of Native American culture and the enslavement of Africans, then why do critics of post-

modernity claim that it is morally and socially bankrupt? The
early development of Lyotard's thought offers an excellent example of what many have attacked as the morally and socially bankrupt nature of postmodernism while his later career displays a
modification of earlier positions and a new concern for justice, or
what Steven Best and Douglas Kellner claim "comes close to liberal reformism, which he reconstructs, however, in a postmodern
fashion" (*Postmodern Theory* 162).

The early work of Lyotard concentrates on the rejection of the
primacy of text, refuting the textualist approach that privileges
text over experience, the senses, and images. His hope was to validate new ways of knowing, ways that had been denigrated by
Western culture's allegiance to the word. This insistence on the
primacy of the text is, of course, not surprising, given the fact that
the history of modern Western culture has its roots in the Judeo-
Christian tradition, a religious tradition whose holy texts often
inscribe its God as the word: "In the beginning was the Word, and
the Word was with God, and the Word was God" (John 1:1). In
his endeavor to subvert this obsession with text, Lyotard, following the philosophical and linguistic line first established by Derrida, asserts that Western philosophy operates around a set of
binary oppositions. Struggling against the tyranny of dichotomous
valuation, Lyotard champions what has been neglected: the figure,
the image, which may only be apprehended through the senses.
Best and Kellner explain that from this position Lyotard develops
a philosophy of desire based heavily on Freudian theory, celebrat-
ing "all desire (positive and negative) for providing intensities of
experience, liberation from repressive conditions, and creativity"
(150). For Lyotard, the function of theory is not only to understand or interpret but also to criticize, to overturn the established
order that some may find intolerable. Best and Kellner contend
that Lyotard was dissatisfied with the conventional boundaries of
criticism: "Criticizing and negating, [Lyotard] suggests, is infinite
and useless, never coming to an end" (153).

Out of these doldrums, Lyotard emerged to embrace what
may be characterized as a "Nietzschean affirmative discourse
within a politics and philosophy of desire" (Best and Kellner 153).
It is within his philosophy of libidinal economy that Lyotard may
be criticized for his lack of concern with justice or morality; at this
point in his career the only goal was the cultivation of the circu-
lation, flows, intensities, and energetics of desire. This cultivation

did not involve a judgment of positive or negative energies but rather focused on desire itself; it is a postmodern perspective that stresses "activities that produce intensities, that free and intensify the flow of desire . . . over modern politics which are concerned with such things as rights and justice" (Best and Kellner 155). Of course, if one is not concerned with such things as rights and justice and instead embraces all of life's intensities, there is the danger that within the free flow of positive and negative energy conditions of an intolerable nature may be produced, conditions that disrupt any cultivation of the very desire Lyotard claims we most need.[15] Best and Kellner suggest that Lyotard's early work pursued a politics of bodily affirmation to its extremes, a position that he eventually saw as limited and limiting; after discovering this blind spot, Lyotard's position modified and moved toward a politics of justice. While Lyotard's early work embraces a desire that he claims exists outside of or beyond good and evil—a position that fails to recognize the danger in not distinguishing between desire that emancipates and desire that confines, between a fascist desire and a revolutionary desire—his later work addresses these very issues.

John McGowan represents the later Lyotard as a neo-pragmatist and suggests that in a work like *Just Gaming*, Lyotard, by focusing on the particularity of rules in language games, opposes any notion of universal rules in our use of language. Like Fish, Rorty, and other pragmatists, Lyotard asserts that language is at all times contextual and communal, and his conclusion about the nature of language games, a conclusion that emphasizes the singular justice of each game, implies "that nothing sets limits to the directions in which the game can go; localism becomes associated with endless 'experimentation,' a highly desirable situation" (McGowan, *Postmodernism* 183). Lyotard employs language games as a way of addressing the politics of justice. Language games are to be seen as representative of the nature of all games, and, of course, life itself, with all its possible realities, is seen as a game. Therefore, the principles of language games, principles that rest paradoxically on a sole prescriptive of universal value that insists on "the observance of the singular justice of each game such as it has just been situated" (Lyotard and Thebaud 100), may apply to other situations, and in this way it is possible to discern contextual justice not just in theory but in daily practice. In a conversation with Jean-Loup Thebaud, Lyotard explains that "Yes, there is

first a multiplicity of justices, each one of them defined in relation
to the rules specific to each game. These rules prescribe what must
be done so that a denotative statement, or an interrogative one, or
a prescriptive one, etc., is received as such and recognized as 'good'
in accordance with the criteria of the game to which it belongs"
(100). Thus, within a game or a local community, there are rules or
criteria that establish prescriptive norms or values in the use of language, and by applying this theoretical paradigm to issues of a
fleshly nature—poststructuralists argue that we may only apprehend "real" issues like poverty or racism or gang violence through
language—these norms or values that are valid at the local level
may be used to define injustice or immorality.

　　But what of communities whose rules we find intolerable?
What do we do when we witness a game outside of our own context whose rules call for racist behavior or fascist violence? Must
we turn away, resigned to the operations of value and morality
within our own community? Without a center of value on which
we may base moral or ethical judgments, are we confined to our
own communities, never to examine or judge the actions of other
nations or cultures? Lyotard's response, of course, would rest on
the theoretical principle that postmodernity allows for the proliferation of stories, refuting any single claim to "truth," and in this
way protecting against any monomaniacal scrambling for control
of others. In other words, if there are conditions a people find rep-
rehensible, then they might simply create new stories, new
"truths," on which to base new community practices. While the-
oretically this appears to be revolutionary, it fails to acknowledge
real principles of power, the workings of capital and war
machines. Although Lyotard's work empowers certain voices that
have been neglected and celebrates multiplicity, it also exposes a
weakness of the postmodern position: If there is no universal
value, no center from which we can establish a set of criteria for
· the human condition, then how can we take political action
against communities whose practices we wish to deem reprehensi-
ble? How do we condemn and combat such heinous acts as "eth-
nic cleansing" in Bosnia or female genital mutilation in various
cultures in Africa? On what basis do we rebuke the terrorist
whose leaders invoke a religious narrative that calls for a holy war
to cleanse the earth of the infidel's heresy.

　　This is perhaps most problematic today as we find our culture
expanding into multiplicities that are at times disturbing to those

who remember the days when it "all made sense," when there was (the illusion of) universal agreement concerning morality and value. Those who long nostalgically for such times—times that include the debacle of McCarthyism—reflect our need for order and consistency and reason, our desire for justice in a universe that too often seems unjust. It is far more simple to live in a world of black and white than one with muted shades of gray. It is much more comforting to believe that the United States is somehow divinely anointed for providential business, to perceive the nation's leaders as somehow beyond reproach, than to recognize the limitations of our national vision and the existence of other national dreams. In the postmodern world, however, this illusion has been shattered and destroyed by a postmodern condition that indefinitely postpones any totality of meaning and produces a proliferation of stories, temporalities, and spaces. The domination of video and audio technology united with a computer industry whose innovations grow exponentially each year continues to produce and reproduce the proliferation of multiplicity that some postmodernists most desire. With television coverage of the House and Senate on C-Span and C-Span 2, for example, it becomes increasingly difficult to hide from the reality that there is no universal consensus on what the United States is or what its position in the world should be; the types of information provided to the consumer in America today are significantly different from those provided to the consumer of the first half of the twentieth century. No longer do we rely on a small number of newspapers or magazines to supply us with a decorous and static story of our nation's hopes and dreams; our exposure to more and more information nudges us toward an epiphany that suggests truth is fluid and ambivalent.

Postmodern theory tends to frustrate our very natural and very real desire for clarity and orderliness. Ihab Hassan contends that "Poststructuralist theory, though full of brio and bravura, can only taunt our desire to make sense. It can only tease us into further thought, not anchor our meanings" (*The Postmodern Turn* 196). Our rather recent move toward a form of postmodern pluralism and the acceptance of relativism by some as a viable philosophical stance shakes the very foundations of our culture or, more exactly, the former foundations to which we look longingly but cannot embrace innocently. The historical and philosophical shifts from the premodern to the modern—characterized by a move away from a universal and totalizing monotheism to a universal and totalizing humanist rationalism that replaced God with man and the miracle of the spirit with the miracle of science—did not prepare us for the disconcerting consequences of postmodernism's radical break toward multiplicity. There is a clear connection between this radical philosophical shift in the contemporary world and the increasing number of religious cults and the fervent new turn to fundamentalist religion—both Christian and Muslim—that we witness in the United States and the Middle East.

Although many postmodern philosophers see the effects of poststructuralism's critique of essence and centrality as an opportunity for negative freedom or endless play, there exists among the masses a reluctance to embrace the postmodern. Humanity does not appear to be in a state of euphoria over the postmodern condition, a condition that offers no facile answers, no clearly delineated lines on which to order existence. Instead we find large groups of people calling for a return to traditional morality, for a belief in the spiritual or mystical. Sadly, at times these groups find the clarity they seek in the company of fascists, racists, and warmongers. In our own country we have seen the tragic consequences of Charles Manson, Jim Jones, and David Koresh, while witnessing the growth of the religious right promulgated by such leaders as Pat Robertson and Jerry Falwell. Not surprisingly, the New Age movement, including the growing furor surrounding angels and astrology and the practice of witchcraft known as Wicca, has been consistently exploited by tabloid television. The sweeping success of the likes of Bill O'Reilly and Rush Limbaugh—as they confidently tell their listeners in no uncertain terms what is right and what is wrong with the political and social spheres in the United States—certainly indicates the seductive appeal of the demagogue to those who wish to have, as Ihab Hassan puts it, meaning anchored.

Outside of the United States the corollary of humanity's desire for univocal meaning appears in the form of religions like Islam and Judaism, faiths practiced fervently in the Middle East, harboring, like Christianity, the potential for intolerance, as well as the ability to incite jihad. Certainly the horror of the destruction of the World Trade Centers on 11 September 2001 is the result of this very kind of desire. Roland Barthes, in an essay entitled "The World of Wrestling," argues that what we most desire is clarity of

justice and morality. Barthes examines what would now be called
professional wrestling and suggests that such an event is no different than a religious ceremony or a Greek drama; "it is the spectacle of excess" (450). In such settings, it is exceedingly clear who
is evil and who is just; the crowd uniformly acknowledges the
grotesque and horrifying nature of evil by verbally haranguing the
wrestler who plays the villain while cheering raucously as good
triumphs. In America, professional wrestling events draw thousands of spectators and even more viewers by television pay-per-
view specials: such events are in high demand in the postmodern
world. Barthes explains that

> In wrestling, nothing exists except in the absolute, there is no
> symbol, no allusion, everything is presented exhaustively. Leav-
> ing nothing in the shade. . . . What is portrayed by wrestling is
> therefore an ideal understanding of things; it is the euphoria of
> men raised for a while above the constitutive ambiguity of every-
> day situations and placed before the panoramic view of a uni-
> vocal Nature, in which signs at last correspond to causes, with-
> out obstacle, without evasion, without contradiction. [It] unveils
> the form of a Justice which is at last intelligible. (53–54)

Events like wrestling represent in perfect detail what Lyotard has
characterized as local knowledge. Professional wrestling creates a
community of shared value; those who come together to watch the
spectacle of excess exhibit a local, contextual, and relational
understanding of good and evil, of just and unjust acts.

The gamut of sporting events that monopolize much of
America's time and money appears to partly satisfy our obsession
with clarity in ways, although repulsive to some, that do not pose
the excessive danger we have witnessed in cults and other fanati-
cal groups. But professional wrestling and other sporting events
present that which life outside the arena does not: swift, unmiti-
gated, rational results. Seldom do we find intelligible justice in
the contemporary world. Therefore, we must return to the central question, one that resists facile dogmatism, demanding serious consideration because of its weighty effect on the way we
conduct the business of living: can we have a source of value that
does not totalize or essentialize—the point of critique of rational
humanist discourse by postmodernists—with the potential to
work beyond the local setting, or are we doomed to micro-poli-

tics, local value, which leaves open the possibilities of injustice in other communities that ultimately may destroy the communities we inhabit? Perhaps one viable answer to an ethical dilemma of such far-reaching consequences may be found in postmodern humanism, a position I argue Vonnegut establishes and modifies over the course of his career.

Postmodern Humanism:
The Issues of Value and Essence

What does it mean to be a postmodern moralist? More to the point, as some critics of postmodernism have challenged, can there be a system of morality, an ethics, if there is no center or essence on which to base it? Such questions—often asked by critics of postmodernism and avoided by its advocates—expose the perplexing dilemma of postmodernity: if, as Zygmunt Bauman argues, "there are no longer any rules or norms to guide inquiry, no overall validity, no universal, unequivocal basis for truth or taste" (197), then how can one make decisions about daily living, an activity that will inevitably include moral conundrums?

Historically, in Western culture, our morality, the system of value on which we have based practices as banal as the removal of waste and as esoteric as the development of the spirit, has been based upon essence or a belief in an ultimate center, often called "God." The very notion of value—entwined at first with the idea of God and, more recently in the modern age, with the idea of the essential goodness of humanity, the perfectibility of the race—undergirds many institutions that continue to control our actions in contemporary daily life. Many postmodernists, however, have moved away from any belief in essence or value, in part because of the radical contradictions found in twentieth-century history and the ensuing disillusionment of philosophers like Foucault, Lyotard, and Baudrillard. Modernist humanism, according to Pauline Marie Rosenau, failed postmodernists in a number of ways, including its justification of Western superiority and its significant role in cultural imperialism (47–49). Such events as World War I and World War II, the Holocaust, the Vietnam War, and Watergate damaged the credibility of humanist claims for the progress of our culture and the heretofore glorified scope of its achievements. How could one believe in humankind as rational in the face of such threats as nuclear destruction and social injustice? Douglas Kellner explains that "the tradition of modern philosophy was destroyed by its vacuous and impossible dreams of a foundation for philosophy, an absolute bedrock of truth that could serve as the guarantee of philosophical systems" ("Postmodernism as Social Theory" 240).

While the destruction of humanism took place in diverse areas of thought throughout the academic community, the rejection of essentialism most notably occurred by storm in the humanities as the work of Paul de Man and Jacques Derrida proliferated. The theoretical project of deconstruction, at its height during the 1980s, has since fallen off; at present, it is recognized as an important step in our movement toward a greater critical awareness, and it is arguably the single most innovative alteration in critical theory in the past half century.[16] Furthermore, this profound and varied infiltration of deconstructive ideas continues to influence our work in such a way that, as Linda Hutcheon explains in "Historiographic Metafiction: Parody and the Intertextuality of History," virtually all theory examining contemporary literature challenges "both closure and single, centralized meaning" (7). The notion that closure and single, centralized meaning must inevitably disappear in aporia certainly is no longer avant-garde; in fact, one need only glance at the many books that offer an overview of our critical field to see that deconstruction and other poststructuralist theories have continually attacked essentialist pronouncements, making it difficult, if not impossible, for the critic to argue for any kind of central meaning or value.

The project of deconstruction, however, is not neutral; the act of critiquing metanarratives and embracing local narratives is an ethical and political process, one of far-ranging consequences. Tobin Siebers, in *The Ethics of Criticism*, contends that deconstruction's "emphasis on the marginal . . . takes on moral overtones in its opposition to relations of power and systematic thought. Deconstructive marginalization has the ethical virtue of siding with the underdog" (98). Deconstruction and other poststructuralist positions attempt to combat all forms of theory, equating systematic thought with the violence of power; such decisive antagonism, however, is itself a political activity with the potential for the same kinds of aggressions and exclusions associated with totalizing metanarratives, and many would argue that deconstruction, in its deference to the marginal, continually excludes numerous possibilities in literary studies, possibilities of potential meaning and connection (Siebers 98–99). Consequently, where does the work of Derrida or de Man leave us? Our position at this theoretical crossroads has not proven satisfactory to all. Ihab Hassan speaks hopefully of a future that may surpass our present devotion to fragmentation, our disdain for wholeness; he implores the reader to work toward a new understanding of creation: "I have no answer. Yet I believe that an answer must go beyond our current shibboleths: disconfirmation, decreation, demystification, deconstruction, decentering, depropriation, difference, etc. Perhaps we need to go beyond Irony (as Nietzsche sometimes did), beyond the current aversion to Wholeness and Meaning, to some working faith in. . . . What?" (*Paracriticisms* xv). This hope that we might transcend our current position—transform what is fragmented into reassociations constructed by the means of a working faith, not by a dogmatic proclamation of our possession of truth but rather by a pragmatic move toward a postmodern "wholeness" that emphasizes the fluid, mutable meaning of human existence—is the crux of postmodern humanism.

As discussed earlier, Lyotard offers one possible solution to Hassan's shibboleths: value and morality may be established within local communities so that the daily questions of living may be addressed from a local center. But what of discourse between communities? How might communities live together in the same nation if their local systems of value are diametrically opposed to one another? Moreover, how might nations live together in the same world if their systems of value are in direct conflict? Lyotard's answer to such difficult and consequential questions appears to ignore the nature of human relations. Lyotard does not tackle the human quandary of living with difference between communities; rather, he acknowledges that the problem exists, calling it the "differend," which he defines as "a case of conflict between (at least) two parties that cannot be equitably resolved for lack of a rule of judgment applicable to both arguments" (*The Differend* xi). But where does the differend leave us? Lyotard does not agonize over this philosophical dilemma because in his purview good postmodernism is never tyrannical, never imposing; remaining within the confines of local communities, it is liberatory in its proliferation of multiplicities. Lyotard, however, appears to ignore the political nature of humanity, its desire for power, for material gain, for control; he neglects the fact that many outside the academic community remain committed to an essentialist worldview. We must not forget that most nations do not embrace pluralism or democracy in any form; many cultures reject the theoretical project of postmodernism, and brutally and violently deter the infiltration of multiplicities. Even in the United States, in a nation whose governmental processes and legislation appear to embrace pluralism more radically than those of almost any other nation, there is an economic system, free enterprise, that simultaneously exploits and deters the proliferation of certain factions.

Clearly the economic control wielded by various American corporations as they move into markets in Mexico, Taiwan, or China, paying the native laborers a fraction of what they would have to pay American laborers, establishes a system of domination that curbs the proliferation of multiplicities. Many critics of postmodernity's consumer culture—building upon the work of Theodor Adorno, who argued that industrial societies, such as our own, undermine critical thought among the population in an effort to further the national economic machinery—claim that postmodernism is conservative in nature, reifying the productions of power that exploit and oppress by transforming that which is marginal into consumer goods; what at first appears to be the positive recognition of local cultures and the assertion that their knowledge is valid, quickly disappears into subtle marketing strategies, well-wrought cogs in the wheel of late capitalism. Fredric Jameson's work, which Haynes Horne argues is motivated by an unmistakably modernist impulse, recognizes the fallibility of Lyotard's position, its susceptibility to the movements of evil, to humanity's historically consistent abuse of power.[17] Horne contends that Jameson wishes to contain the poststructuralist program described by Lyotard, that "the radical dissolution of metanarratives which Lyotard describes can only be endorsed when this dissolution functions within programs" (272). Jameson acknowledges the lure of the poststructuralist critique. Although the deconstruction of metanarratives empowers the marginalized, it also strips them of any political power based on essence, and, for Jameson, who aspires to meld postmodernism with Marxism in an effort to battle late capitalism, this proves to be a devastating blow.

While I agree with Jameson's notion that the poststructuralist critique should be harnessed, I do not wish to suggest that this must inevitably lead back to essentialist or totalizing narratives. Poststructuralism, if practiced without purpose, tenders little beyond the shibboleths of which Hassan speaks; left uncontained, such work only appears to lead to fragmentation and, perhaps, eventually to anarchy. If we are to accept Tobin Siebers's claim that "literary criticism affects the relation between literature and human life" (2), then, as we practice poststructuralist criticism, we should have an eye toward its effects on the human condition. The work of Douglas Kellner offers one possible paradigm by which we may approach the shibboleths of the postmodern condition, one that may bridge the divide that looms between modernity and post-modernity. In a lecture entitled, "Critical Theory vs. Postmodern Theory: Contemporary Debates in Social Theory," Kellner claims that in order adequately to address the needs of contemporary thought, we must use both modern and postmodern theory. Kellner, whose work derives in part from the Frankfurt School tradition, argues that we need both postmodernism's critique of meta-narratives and its subsequent attention to disunity and fragmentation, as well as modernity's hopeful attempts to create infinitely new unities or reassociations. The tradition of the Frank-furt School affords Kellner a normative base of value on which he grounds political and social action, while postmodern theory insists that these norms cannot be totalized. This balance between the need for a normative base and a rejection of essentializing or totalizing narratives has been key in opening areas of criticism, like multiculturalism or feminism, forms of criticism that use literature and criticism to effect physical and social change.[18] Kellner's use of the modern and postmodern also points toward the paradox of postmodern humanism, a position that affirms humanistic values while maintaining a postmodern perspective.

Even though postmodernism calls into question the very idea of a unified, essential subject, the postmodern subject nonetheless lives pragmatically as if the grand narratives of the past remain firmly intact. When we speak of love or hate in our relationships, of the oppression of racism or the liberating freedom of tolerance, we do so using a modernist model of the individual subject; appar-ently, despite the claims of postmodern theorists, we continue to posit essence or value with the individual subject, a practice with clear benefits. Perhaps the best satiric example of "living" post-modern theory, an activity seldom encountered, may be found in *Nice Work*, one of several academic novels written by David

Lodge. In this novel, Lodge jabs humorously at the inane absurdity that postmodern theory can be translated directly into the physical actions of contemporary daily life.[19] After Vic Wilcox, an industrial manager, and Robyn Penrose, an English professor whose work involves postmodern feminist theory, finish making love for the first time, Vic announces his devotion to Robyn. Robyn is shocked by his display and attempts to deconstruct a situation that she sees as merely the effects of language and biology:

> "I've been in love with you for weeks."
> "There's no such thing," she says. "It's a rhetorical device. It's a bourgeois fallacy."
> "Haven't you ever been in love, then?"
> "When I was younger," she says, "I allowed myself to be constructed by the discourse of romantic love for a while, yes."
> "What the hell does that mean?"
> "We aren't essences, Vic. We aren't unique individual essences existing prior to language. There is only language."
> "What about this?" he says, sliding his hand between her legs.
> "Language and biology," she says, opening her legs wider. "Of course we have bodies, physical needs and appetites. My muscles contract when you touch me there—feel?"
> "I feel," he says.
> "And that's nice. But the discourse of romantic love pretends that your finger and my clitoris are extensions of two unique individual selves who need each other and only each other and cannot be happy without each other for ever and ever." (210)

In this passage, Lodge satirizes the totalizing claims of poststructuralism, while in the novel as a whole he seems to suggest that the essentialist world of Vic and the nonessentialist world of Robyn may be wed in such a manner that both parties benefit. The wedding of these worlds is the project of postmodern humanism. In *Deliberate Criticism: Toward a Postmodern Humanism*, Stephen R. Yarbrough contends that what we need in order to create a humanism for the postmodern world is a communal sense. Using the work of Friedrich Nietzsche, Martin Heidegger, Jean-Paul Sartre, and Irving Babbitt, Yarbrough argues that humanism does not always express a belief in the idea of a fixed human nature, a point of contention for postmodernists. Rather, Yarbrough claims that "we must learn how to assert the center, for the center itself, unlike the concrete aims from which we choose our courses of action, must be willed into place. It is, in short, a master convention" (37). Yarbrough, however, remains unclear about exactly what may be willed into place. Like so many other postmodern philosophers who desire to ground their discourse, Yarbrough cannot point with any authority to the common ground of which he speaks longingly, a ground on which discourse between cultures may be built.

But Vonnegut is another matter. He offers a hopeful solution to the postmodern condition. In his novels, speeches, and essays, he presents the potential for reassociations, for creation, for a world beyond fragmentation. To understand Vonnegut's propitious postmodern humanism, we must first briefly outline the major tenets of modernist humanism. Modernist humanism may be characterized best by examining the center of its discourse which is the human subject. According to Robert Merrill, in his foreword to *Ethics/Aesthetics: Post-Modern Positions*, modernist humanism draws all cognitive, aesthetic, and ethical maps to the scale of the individual subject who believes in the originality and individuality of a unified self (xi–xiii). The modern subject defines the rest of the world as Other and posits meaning in this Other only in its relation to the self. This had profound effects, of course, on the modernist subject's apprehension of other cultures and what has been seen by many, in the postmodern era, as the oppression of those cultures unlike our own, as well as the unflinching destruction of entire ecosystems that at the time of their ruin seemed far removed from individual human needs. But, at present, to deny the value of the individual subject, given the nature of Western discourse, would also be ineffective. Even in the postmodern, or, perhaps, especially in the postmodern, the personal and individual continue to captivate.[20] Therefore, while postmodern humanism denies an essential individuality to the subject, it does not disregard the value of human life. Rather, postmodern humanism exalts all life, recognizing the global associations of humanity and its intricately delicate alliance with the earth; Vonnegut's own vision has expanded over the course of his career to encompass such a delicate alliance, and his postmodern humanism offers Merrill a provisional answer—for any postmodern response must remain provisional—a possibility for an existence beyond binary opposition, a morality that is negotiated on an operational essentialism in much the same way Stephen Slemon has shown post-colonial texts "working towards 'realism' within an awareness of referential slippage" (434). In other words, postmodern humanism works with an awareness of its own constructedness toward a symbolic construction of a better "reality." This better reality, however, remains devoted to humanity, and some might argue that such a valuing of human life is actually no different from modernist humanism. The postmodern devotion to humanity, however, runs counter to modernist humanism in its motivation. While modernist humanism espoused its desire to improve or perfect humanity based on the idea of each individual's unique and univocal self, postmodern humanism wishes to better the human condition because of the relative worth of all life and the potential that such life may hold in its proliferation of multiplicities. For the modern humanist, the focus was utopia, an end result based on the belief in the perfectibility of humanity; for the postmodern humanist, there can be no utopia, only endless play, endless affirmation of life. Unlike the modernist, the postmodernist does not believe in the perfectibility of humanity or a final, static position such as utopia; rather, the postmodern humanist concentrates on daily, local activity that may improve human life.[21]

Perhaps the most significant difference between modern and postmodern humanism is the transparency of postmodern humanism. Postmodern humanism openly acknowledges that, in the absence of a "given" center of value, it creates a center of value, that it constructs a position that reveres all life. Unlike historic Western European discourse that first placed value on human life because of its belief that humanity was created in the image of God, postmodernism feigns no assurance that "truth" may be founded on the knowledge of providence or science or any other grand narrative that wishes to establish itself as the essence or center on which discourse may be grounded. The differences between modern humanism and postmodern humanism finally boil down to the issue of essence: one believes in a fixed, essential reference while the other, dismissing this notion, offers only an operational essentialism.

In an interview, Vonnegut claims that "everything is a lie, because our brains are two-bit computers, and we can't get very high-grade truths out of them. But as far as improving the human condition goes, our minds are certainly up to that. That's what they were designed to do. And we do have the freedom to make up comforting lies. But we don't do enough of it" (Allen, *Conversations* 77). In Vonnegut's terms, postmodern humanism is nothing more than a comforting lie, one more constructed narrative in the infinite range of narratives. Moreover, postmodern humanism confesses that it is entirely based on faith; it presupposes that human life is valuable, and it does so with no means to validate such a claim. As Vonnegut, who is the honorary president of the American Humanist Association, explains in *God Bless You, Dr. Kevorkian*, "If it weren't for the message of mercy and pity in Jesus's Sermon on the Mount, I wouldn't want to be a human being. I would just as soon be a rattlesnake" (10). And like his great-grandfather, Clemens Vonnegut, he doesn't have to have the rational or dogmatic proof that so many Enlightenment thinkers find essential. Vonnegut points to Clemens's assertion that "If what Jesus said was good, what can it matter whether he was God or not?" (10). Like his German freethinking ancestors who resided in Indianapolis, Vonnegut cannot rationally prove that mercy is the greatest good or that Jesus was indeed God made flesh. Instead he places his faith in a narrative that does not argue for the existence of God—he explains that "humanists, having received no credible information about any sort of God, are content to serve as well as they can, the only abstraction with which they have some familiarity: their communities" (11). Vonnegut's faith is rooted in the idea of mercy for fellow humans and for the planet itself. In short, the constructed center or provisional metanarrative of Vonnegut's postmodern humanism is the idea that life is precious, and every attempt should be made to improve the conditions of life in order to preserve it.

In a speech to the graduating class of Bennington College in 1970, Vonnegut both implored the new graduates to accept the program of postmodern humanism and displayed the constructedness of such a program: "I beg you to believe in the most ridiculous superstition of all: that humanity is at the center of the universe, the fulfiller or the frustrator of the grandest dreams of God Almighty. If you can believe that, and make others believe it, then there might be hope for us. Human beings might stop treating each other like garbage, might begin to treasure and protect each other instead" (Wampeters 163–64). As a postmodern moralist, Vonnegut centers his discourse on what I have called postmodern humanism, and from this vantage he applauds any action that enhances life and condemns any action that causes suffering or destruction of life. Vonnegut is a self-proclaimed moralist, and, as such, he ardently works to get his message across: "So now when I speak to students, I do moralize. I tell them not to take more than they need, not to be greedy," Vonnegut explains. "I tell them not to kill, even in self-defense. I tell them not to pollute water or the atmosphere. I tell them not to raid the public treasury. I tell them not to work for people who pollute water or the atmosphere, or who raid the public treasury. I tell them not to commit war crimes or to help others to commit war crimes. These morals go over very well" (*Wampeters* 100). Vonnegut creates many possible answers, small narratives or "comforting lies," based on the over-arching construct of postmodern humanism in response to the shibboleths of the postmodern condition. His work flies in the face of those who argue that postmodernity is at best vacuous and amoral and at worst immoral. By examining both the develop-ment of Vonnegut's postmodern critique of America's grand nar-ratives and his moral or ethical system based on postmodern humanism, we will better understand his ever-growing oeuvre and the true importance of his work as a postmodern moralist.

Ethical Criticism: Inroads to
Vonnegut's Postmodern Humanism

Wayne Booth, in his prodigious *The Company We Keep: An Ethics of Fiction*, suggests that ethical criticism, because of its mis-use in the past to censor and repress all kinds of literature deemed immoral by some, fell on hard times and was replaced by various formalist theories that ignored the very real ethical or political effects of literature. In recent decades, however, ethical criticism has made a comeback of sorts, motivated, in part, by the work of "feminist critics asking embarrassing questions about a male-dominated literary canon and what it has done to the 'conscious-ness' of both men and women; by black critics pursuing . . . ques-tion[s] about racism in American classics; by neo-Marxists exploring class biases in European literary traditions; by religious critics attacking modern literature for its 'nihilism' or 'atheism'" (Booth 5). Although much of the modern era denied the political or ethical nature of literature, claiming that in some mystical fash-ion art transcended the boundaries of politics or ethics, postmod-ern philosophy has demonstrated the folly in such a claim, arguing that art is indeed political, a product of societal mores and power relations. The mispractice of ethical criticism has usually involved acts of judgment that in essence imply the work is somehow inferior because of its system of morality; such criticism, reductive in nature, often leads to censorship and produces no fruitful scholarship. What Booth, among others, wishes to establish is a form of criticism that examines a work of art in order to discover and make explicit the moral sensibility informing that work. In *On Moral Fiction*, John Gardner argued that moral criticism is absolutely necessary for the health of English studies, and, despite his often sweeping generalizations about the value of certain artists, *On Moral Fiction* must be acknowledged as an important precursor to the revival of contemporary interest in ethical criticism. Gardner's rage against the English academy was fueled by his belief that the study of literature had become morally bankrupt, completely uninterested in what is most human about literature. Before his untimely death in 1982, Gardner used his influence as a noted writer of fiction and as a professor of English in an effort to sway the tide of intellectual thought toward an affirmation of the mystery and beauty of life.[22]

If we are to accept the proposition that literature reflects human experience while at the same time it affects human experience, that literature is both a product of the social order and helps establish and maintain that social order, it becomes clear that, in its desire to examine the moral and ethical nature of a work of art, ethical criticism establishes an important bond between the life of the text and the life of the reader. This bond, however, should never be viewed facilely or reductively. Patricia Meyer Spacks contends that while fictional narratives offer opportunities for ethical reflection, they are not imperatives for behavior; rather, according to Spacks, "paradigms of fiction provide an opportunity for moral playfulness: cost-free experimentation" (203). While it is true that reading offers, above all, the possibility of experience, or what Spacks explains is the "experience of agency or its illusion" (203), one must never forget that those experiences acquired through the act of reading—although powerful and affecting—should not be feared or repressed. Rather, the act of reading may be understood as an activity that affords experimentation, the trying on of new possibilities without the finality or consequences of life outside of reading. To the detriment of ethical criticism, in the past too many critics have used this form of reading as a tool for censorship in order to imprison works whose moral systems conflicted with their own. Reductive and confining, such behavior has no clear benefit in the discipline of literary studies. Moreover, what we have witnessed as a result of such censorious behavior is a backlash against ethical criticism, an attempt to constrain this kind of work in literary studies, to bar critics from engaging in an activity that tenders potentially profitable readings, readings that connect our study of texts with the physical world beyond the texts.[23]

Robert Coles, a professor of psychiatry and medical humanities at Harvard University, argues with great passion for work that explores literature in an attempt to uncover issues of an ethical or moral nature. Suggesting that such study makes important contributions to daily living beyond the classroom walls, Coles contends that "Students need more opportunity for moral and social reflection on the problems that they have seen at first hand. . . . Students need the chance to directly connect books to experience" (A64). As Kenneth Womack and I suggest in our preface to *Mapping the Ethical Turn*, "to pretend that the ethical or moral dimensions of the human condition were abandoned or obliterated in the shift to postmodernity certainly seems naïve. Part of being human involves the daily struggle with the meanings and consequences of our actions, a struggle most often understood in narrative structures as we tell others and ourselves about what has transpired or what we fear will transpire in the future" (ix).

For the purposes of this study, then, ethical criticism offers unique avenues to the examination of Vonnegut's postmodern humanism. The form of ethical criticism I wish to undertake has nothing to do with dogmatic judgments or prescriptive moralizing. Ethical criticism that attempts to censor, to limit the parameters of intellectual exploration, does violence not only to the literary work but to intellectual curiosity as well; it offers little more than the safety of stasis. By contrast, this study offers a form of ethical criticism that attempts to examine the ideas of value and morality— ideas that have long been neglected by formalist criticism to the detriment of the English academy—in ways that allow us to elucidate the patterns of Vonnegut's ethical universe. The importance of such a study lies in the postmodern vision of Vonnegut himself, a way of seeing that presents the possibilities for the affirmation and creation of new life in an age that has too often embraced the shibboleths of deconstruction instead of the possible unities that lie beyond: the hope for a viable humanism in the postmodern world.

2

Searching for Answers in the Early Novels

Or, What Are We Here for Anyway?

Everyone now knows how to find the meaning of life within himself. But mankind wasn't always so lucky. Less than a century ago men and women did not have easy access to the puzzle boxes within them. They could not name even one of the fifty-three portals to the soul.
—Kurt Vonnegut, *The Sirens of Titan*

Daydreaming about God:
Vonnegut as Philosophical Novelist

BEFORE LOOKING AT Vonnegut's initial forays into the fictional long form, I suggest that some understanding of the impetus behind his artistry is in order. Without a clear grasp of Vonnegut's intellectual heritage and his own financial and familial situation, we may not discern why a former soldier, college dropout, and public relations writer left his steady job at General Electric in order to write novels that are forever preoccupied with the meaning of our existence. As Vonnegut tells it, his decision to become a writer had less to do with some mythical yearning to express the mystery of the human condition and more to do with the kinds of money he was able to earn in the short story market. In an interview with Charles Reilly, Vonnegut describes his amazement upon receiving his first check for a short story published in *Collier's*:

> There I was making ninety-two bucks a week with two kids to support, and out of nowhere comes a check for $750. Two months take-home pay! . . . Needless to say, this caused me to do a bit of thinking about my life-role at General Electric. I wrote another story right away, and this time they paid me $900, because they would give you regular raises to keep you producing. Pretty soon I had money piling up in the corridors and I resigned from General Electric. (Allen, *Conversations* 198)

This would seem an odd and inauspicious beginning for an author who twenty years later captivated a nation with an important book about the atrocity of war and the nature of time, if it were not for his cultural heritage and his indefatigable and, at times, insolent curiosity.

Hearing Vonnegut tell the story of his beginnings as a writer, we might be led to think criticisms of his fiction as hackwork are, at least in part, justified. But we must not lose sight of Vonnegut's droll humor and self-deprecating ways. Moreover, if Vonnegut were to recount his rite of passage as a fledgling writer in terms of some beatific moment of inspiration, we would surely be wary that this postmodern harlequin was indeed guiding us toward some punch line. Certainly financial woes were an integral force in shaping the career of this—like many another—American author, but the radical break from traditional philosophical thought exhibited even in his earliest fiction cannot be attributed to his desire to please magazine editors at *Collier's* or the *Saturday Evening Post*. Rather, Vonnegut's turn to writing and his preoccupation with matters of religion result from his unconventional and unorthodox family heritage. Vonnegut's ancestry, while rooted in Midwestern life, remains an anomaly when compared to the experience of most Midwestern families at the turn of the century. Vonnegut himself has noted on several occasions in interviews and essays that his family's religious skepticism and their love of the arts is likely the most significant force behind his work: "[Religious skepticism] is my ancestral religion. How it was passed on to me is a mystery. . . . How proud I became of our belief, how pigheadedly proud, even, is the most evident thing in my writing, I think" (*Palm Sunday* 194–95). With great enthusiasm, he recites his family's list of accomplishments in Indianapolis, explaining that art, architecture, beer-brewing, and even writing held prominent positions in his home and the homes of his relatives. His mother, who committed suicide when Vonnegut was twenty-two years old, attempted to support the family by writing after the failure of the family's architectural business, and Vonnegut regards her work positively, although "she had no talent for the vulgarity the slick magazines required" (Allen, *Conversations* 178). The devotion to artistic creation witnessed by Vonnegut from early childhood helps explain, in part, his turn to writing as a way not only to support his family but also to fill the void of existence with the life only artistic creation provides. When we consider his father's architectural designs in Indianapolis or his later work as an artist of rural landscapes in Brown County, Indiana, and his mother's considerable education, her talk of travels in Europe and its many treasures, or her final attempts to write what never could sell in the magazines of the day, it is far easier to understand Vonnegut's ambitious turn to storytelling.

The Vonnegut family's devotion to artistic creation, however, does not explain fully Vonnegut's fascination with philosophical questions. In order to puzzle out this conundrum, we must turn to Vonnegut's great-grandfather, Clemens Vonnegut, who wrote an *Instruction in Morals* published in 1900. Although Clemens Vonnegut was raised a Roman Catholic, he is often characterized as a freethinker and a religious skeptic. Vonnegut explains that he aspires to be the "cultivated eccentric" that his great-grandfather was, and Vonnegut's own morality, demonstrated with great diversity and fervor in his writing, clearly owes much to his ancestor. In a fitting tribute to his great-grandfather, Vonnegut uses the following quotation from his treatise on morality for the epigraph to *Palm Sunday*: "Whoever entertains liberal views and chooses a consort that is captured by superstition risks his liberty and his happiness" (xix). Like Clemens, Vonnegut continually resists any consort who dabbles in beliefs based on superstition, and his writing, arguably his most trusted companion, continually disparages any belief system that does not hold all humanity's good as its highest calling. In a letter to the dean of the chapel at Transylvania University, Vonnegut describes his own religious conviction in relation to his family's: "I am a fourth generation

German American religious skeptic. Like my essentially puritani-
cal forebears, I believe that God has so far been unknowable and
hence unservable, hence the highest service one can perform is to
his or her community, whose needs are quite evident" (*Fates* 238).
The similarity between Vonnegut's hope to serve humanity and the
following admonition from Clemens Vonnegut is uncanny; in fact,
when *Palm Sunday* first appeared many scholars thought Vonnegut's claim that his great-grandfather had written the piece was
bogus: "Be aware of this truth that the people on this earth could
be joyous, if only they would live rationally and if they would contribute mutually to each others' welfare" (*Palm Sunday* 193).
Although Vonnegut's own views of humanity's ability to live rationally shift significantly during his career, he still abides by the concept that humanity's highest calling must be to serve one another.
Surprisingly, Vonnegut was not aware of Clemens Vonnegut as a
writer until late in life; his brother Bernard sent him a copy of
Clemens's funeral address, as well as *Instruction in Morals*, while
he was preparing *Palm Sunday* in 1979. Therefore, what some
have characterized as Vonnegut's radical departure from religion
and others as a form of postmodern atheism actually appears to
be a continuation and not a break from his own family's practices.
As he explained in an interview with *Playboy*, "My ancestors,
who came to the United States a little before the Civil War, were
atheists. So I'm not rebelling against organized religion. I never
had any. I learned my outrageous opinions about organized religion at my mother's knee" (Allen, *Conversations* 78).

While it may be true that Vonnegut is not rebelling against organized religion, religion, in its broadest sense, remains at the center
of his discourse, and his musing over our existence ultimately presents some form of solace. Solace, Vonnegut claims, is what people
search for in religion; it is the channel for appeasing our frustration,
created to some degree by our inability to know with any assurance
whether there is a God and what our purpose for existence might
be. In a sermon Vonnegut delivered at St. Clement's Episcopal
Church on Palm Sunday in 1980, he claims that "People don't come
to church for preachments, of course, but to daydream about God"
(*Palm Sunday* 330). The same may be said of Vonnegut's work. His
fiction, whether set in Midland City, Ohio, or on the planet
Tralfamadore, continues a long-standing tradition among the Vonneguts: the playful act of daydreaming about God.

Player Piano: After the American Dream

When *Player Piano* first appeared in 1952, little fanfare accompanied it. The first effort from an author who previously had published only a handful of short stories in magazines such as *Collier's* and the *Saturday Evening Post* nearly went unnoticed, and most likely would have escaped any sort of critical attention if the book had not been printed by Charles Scribner's Sons. Indeed, the small number of reviews that appeared were not nearly as scathing as those that followed some of Vonnegut's work more than twenty years later. *Player Piano*, judging by the reviews, might be considered the pinnacle of Vonnegut's career when juxtaposed with the highly publicized attacks on *Breakfast of Champions* or *Slapstick*. Nevertheless, critics had little to say beyond the obvious; comparisons to Orwell's *1984* or Huxley's *Brave New World* were plentiful, and such comparisons, of course, continually found Vonnegut's imitation wanting. Paul Pickrel, in a critique of no more than a paragraph for the *Yale Review*, described *Player Piano* as "the best humorous book I have read in some time" but "not so mordant or so powerful as *Brave New World* or *1984*" (20). In similar fashion, Charles Lee of the *Saturday Review* characterized Vonnegut's first work as "wanting in Orwellian depth, but . . . macabrely playful" (11). Not surprisingly, such comments tell us more about Lee and Pickrel than about *Player Piano*.

While clearly Vonnegut's first novel owes much to Huxley and Orwell, a comparison seems to offer little insight into Vonnegut's own peculiar vision. Vonnegut, like Huxley and Orwell, concerns himself with science and sociology, but the manner in which he approaches his subject differs so radically from his precursors that to speak of their work in the same breath is oxymoronic. The more than half century that has passed since the publication of *Player Piano* affords us the critical hindsight necessary to discern the absurdly satiric nature of Vonnegut's social criticism. The seeds of postmodern thought beginning to sprout even in this, his first novel, are truly revolutionary when measured against the modernist ideas of Orwell and Huxley. Moreover, the nature of Vonnegut's postmodernism exhibits the most basic tenet of Lyotard's celebrated definition of postmodernity: an incredulity toward grand narratives.

Beginning with *Player Piano* and continuing to the present in such works as *Fates Worse Than Death* and *Timequake*, Vonnegut labors to debunk our notions of truth, or as he puts it in *Cat's Cradle*, a novel that questions the validity of religious narratives,

> Tiger got to hunt,
> Bird got to fly;
> Man got to sit and wonder, "Why, why, why?"
> Tiger got to sleep,
> Bird got to land;
> Man got to tell himself he understand. (124)

Humanity may have to reassure itself of its understanding of the nature of things, but Vonnegut humorously undercuts the validity of that understanding. It is humanity's desire for assurance that Vonnegut points to as the cause for grand narratives, but his understanding does not soften his scathing attacks. Long before Derrida and the theoretical project of deconstruction reached its peak in English departments in American universities, Vonnegut subverted the structures of his culture, as he showed the absence of any real center behind the truth espoused in worker manuals and newspapers, in the speeches of CEOs and ministers.

Player Piano is set against the industrial environment of the near future, one that closely resembles Vonnegut's own experience in the corporate world from 1947 to 1950 at General Electric in Schenectady, New York. Paul Proteus, the son of Dr. George Proteus, who at the time of his death was the nation's first National Industrial, Commercial, Communications, Foodstuffs, and Resources Director, serves as the protagonist of the novel. The content of Vonnegut's first novel foreshadows the latent postmodern themes of the author, but its form remains conventionally modernist. In the novel's action we see Paul begin to question and finally struggle against the metanarrative his father helped to establish. The master narrative of *Player Piano* is a myth common to America and often reified in the genre of utopian science fiction: Mechanical progress means a better future for all.[1] Vonnegut was intimately involved in the continued efforts by industry to put this kind of narrative out to the public. As a public relations writer for General Electric, he was paid to find new ways of convincing the public that the work done by industrial corporations was ultimately a step toward a brighter future, a universal good. In 1973, at the height of Vonnegut's popular acclaim, *Playboy* published one of his General Electric press releases from 1950:

> Powerful atom smashers, special motors to drive a supersonic wind tunnel, and calculating machines for solving in minutes problems ordinarily requiring months were among the accomplishments of General Electric engineers during 1949, according to a summary released by the company here today. (229)

Each line of the release strengthens and furthers the American master narrative of progress, pushing for a future where machines may solve problems in nanoseconds, a future that implies comfort for all. And it is this seamlessly created future, a constructed idea with no more truth than any other rhetorical structure, that Vonnegut satirizes in his initial novel. It appears that Vonnegut is worried by the claims of scientists who see themselves, as he put it in a *Playboy* interview with David Standish, "simply unearthing truth," a truth that "could never hurt human beings" (70). Vonnegut continues: "Many scientists were that way—and I've known a hell of a lot of them, because at General Electric, I was a PR man largely for the research laboratory. . . . And back then, around 1949, they were all innocent, all simply dealing with truth and not worried about what might be done with their discoveries" (97). These comments underscore Vonnegut's growing concern with the nature of truth, his misgivings about a truth thought somehow pure, innocent, and essential. While *Player Piano* attempts to expose the philosophical impossibility of some innocent, essential truth, it also reflects Vonnegut's morality. Ever a pragmatist, Vonnegut espouses a morality that reflects his attention to the results, not the process of philosophical inquiry; he is more troubled by the damage to human life caused by our belief in grand narratives than by our clear desire for them.

Unlike other critics, however, who argue that Vonnegut looks longingly toward a simpler past in *Player Piano* and that his answer to industrial progress is nostalgic, I contend that the novel undercuts those metanarratives most important to the social and economic fabric of America. Paul, as he begins to see the flaws in the corporate narrative—the facade of the Meadows session with its rituals praising a world where "civilization has reached the dizziest heights of all time!" (209), never considering how this grand narrative sounds to those laborers living across the river whose skills are no longer needed—for a short time looks nostalgically to the past, more specifically, to other grand narratives of his culture found in novels. We are told that Paul "had never been a reading man, but now he was developing an appetite for novels wherein the hero lived vigorously and out-of-doors, dealing directly with nature, dependent upon basic cunning and physical strength for survival" (135). Paul does not naively accept what he reads: "He knew his enjoyment of them was in a measure childish, and he doubted that a life could ever be as clean, hearty, and satisfying as those in the books. Still and all, there was a basic truth underlying the tales, a primitive ideal to which he could aspire" (135). Ultimately, even this primitive ideal is undercut in the form of the agrarian myth. Paul's hope that he and his wife can be isolated on the Gottwald farm, that they may simply turn from the dominant narrative of Ilium and return to an edenic state where crops were raised by hand and where truthful innocence ethereally emerged from the earth, is undercut with finality in the following passage: "Paul had gone to his farm once, and, in the manner of a man dedicating his life to God, he'd asked Mr. Haycox to put him to work, guiding the hand of Nature. The hand he grasped so fervently, he soon discovered, was coarse and sluggish, hot and wet and smelly. . . . He hadn't gone back" (246).[2] In short, Vonnegut deconstructs the metanarratives of marriage, corporate life, progress, rural life, and revolutionary change. Paul sees, at novel's end, that all are constructed; no part of reality is experienced innocently, essentially. If *Player Piano* followed the pattern of other modernist narratives of dystopian satire, such as Orwell's *1984* or Huxley's *Brave New World*, then at novel's end we would somehow be led to believe that Paul holds the key to society's problems even if he is in some way powerless to enact the necessary changes. But we are not led that way. Rather, we find Paul being used as a pawn by a revolution whose narrative is as faulty and tarnished as that of the corporation. As Paul stands with the revolutionaries, expected to make his own toast to the future, he realizes that all attempts to establish essentialist hierarchies must fail: "'To a better world,' he started to say, but cut the toast short, thinking of the people of Ilium, already eager to recreate the same old nightmare" (320). Ultimately, *Player Piano* offers no grand narrative to replace those that have been deconstructed; there is only the awareness that truth remains no more than a construct, a most unusual idea to be found in a popular novel in 1952.

While *Player Piano* seems to end on a note of despondency as Paul marches off under Lasher's pointed gun, we cannot ignore Vonnegut's intrusions. Even in his first novel, Vonnegut does not appear to be concerned with hiding his own ideas, his own voice. In an interview, Vonnegut suggests that ideas are the driving force behind all books and that the communication of those ideas by writers with strong and enduring conviction constitutes the chief good of literary art. This is not to say that Vonnegut ignores form or stylistic artistry in order to communicate clearly. On the contrary, as his career progresses, form becomes increasingly more significant to the communication of his ideas. Vonnegut explains that we "read this book with good ideas or that book with good ideas until that's where we get our ideas. We don't think them; we read them in books. I like Utopian talk, speculation about what our planet should be, anger about what our planet is. I think writers are the most important members of society, not just potentially but actually. Good writers must have and stand by their own ideas" (Allen, *Conversations* 166).

Vonnegut's ideas concerning the nature of fiction are well-suited to the most contemporary discussions of literary texts. His recognition of the political work inevitably enacted by texts displays a remarkable thoughtfulness, one which portends the destruction of formal barriers later in his career. Quite early in his writing life, Vonnegut recognized the ideological nature of the work he undertook, and his ideas about the nature of truth and the structure of our culture are clearly presented in his first novel. At the conclusion of *Player Piano*, we are left without any doubt that truth is illusive and that the future offers no miraculous elixir leading to utopia. The ethical center of the book refuses to place its faith in any grand narrative, especially the narrative of technological progress in which humanity is divided and made obsolete by machines. But the apparent note of despondency to which some critics point, claiming that Vonnegut's vision is comprised of a dark existentialism, does not account for the words of Paul Proteus as he speaks from the witness stand near the novel's conclusion. As Paul sits before the courtroom—wires attached at strategic points to his body, then running back to a gray cabinet housing a machine with the ability to detect whether he tells the truth or not—he is asked to tell a lie and then a truth so that the machine may be tested for its accuracy. Paul's lie mimics Vonnegut's own negative views about the use of scientific knowledge: "Every new piece of scientific knowledge is a good thing for humanity" (273). The machine, of course, recognizes Paul's lie, as does the reader, who Vonnegut has coaxed toward this conclusion through the first 270 pages of the novel. Even more straightforward is Paul's statement of truth that condenses Vonnegut's own moral anthem to a single sentence: "The main business of humanity is to do a good job of being human beings, not to serve as appendages to machines, institutions, and systems" (273). Vonnegut's message rings with clarity and strength, and the reader recognizes that while the American dream has failed, there may still be hope and purpose for our existence. Vonnegut insists that attending to the business of humanity, although considered trite and simplistic by some, must be our focus.

But how far does Vonnegut's admonition "to do a good job of being human beings" carry us? Many critics have attacked Vonnegut's morality as sentimental balderdash, a sugar pill for an ominous future. Such interpretations, however, neglect the considerable turns each novel takes before arriving at its position. Vonnegut's unflinching and uncompromising presentation of humanity's past performance and his prediction for our collective fate are not ameliorated by his hopeful pronouncements that critics have characterized as purely sentimental. In fact, Vonnegut's work without the possibilities of love or friendship he proffers would suggest a radically different worldview, one that might be described as distanced from what is most human. Indeed, even though Vonnegut admits that "there is an almost intolerable sentimentality beneath everything I write" (*Wampeters* xxv), there is no admission that such sentiment must be viewed pejoratively. The sentiments of love or respect or commitment that break through in Vonnegut's work appear like flashes of light against an ever-darkening sky. Such an appeal to sentiment is quite possibly Vonnegut's own reaction to a culture turned hyperrational by its trust in science, and, as Vonnegut has said on several occasions, such trust was radically undermined by humanity's bungling efforts in its turn to nuclear war. Therefore, although *Player Piano* offers a possible solution to our dilemma as we face a future where being human may not be necessary, the story as a whole remains a sober satire. Vonnegut hopes for change, but he is not fool enough to hold his breath.

His is a cry or, more accurately, a disconcerting laugh against the outrageous actions of a culture that so values material progress that it is willing to forfeit humanity.

Robert Scholes argues that in Vonnegut's work, as in his contemporaries', "we do not find the rhetoric of moral certainty, which has generally been a distinguishing characteristic of the satirical tradition" (*Critical Essays* 82). This lack of moral certainty, however, does not stop Vonnegut from moralizing; rather, it changes the manner of that moralizing. Scholes's conception of satire is based on a modernist criteria. While Vonnegut lacks a rhetoric of moral certainty, he does not lack a moral rhetoric. This lack of certainty is the result of Vonnegut's disillusionment with the utopian claims of nationalism and science, making it virtually impossible for him to argue for a specific ideology or program of morality. As we will see, Vonnegut's war experience, his family's tribulations, and the unraveling of the American dream in the face of McCarthyism and Vietnam, go a long way to explain his reticence toward some prescriptive morality. Therefore, his is a provisional answer to the question of existence, a gesture that lacks specificity but not sincerity, and, although it is not clear what comes after the American dream, it is unequivocally clear that for Vonnegut it must involve the difficult job of being human.

The Sirens of Titan: Vonnegut's Cosmological Wanderings

After the appearance of *Player Piano*, Vonnegut did not publish another novel for seven years. During this time, he continued to write and publish short stories, but his main business involved making ends meet for a family that was growing and changing in unusually tragic ways. *Player Piano* did not make the financial or critical splash for which its author had hoped, and, two years later, Vonnegut found himself teaching English at the Hopefield School on Cape Cod.[3] The school was designed to serve students with special needs, or, as Vonnegut puts it: "It was a school for disturbed kids—disturbed rich kids since it cost a lot of money to go there—in Sandwich, on Cape Cod. I was the whole English department for kids who were of high school age, many of whom could not read or write very much. . . . There were brain-damaged kids and all sorts of kids who had something wrong with them"

(Allen, *Conversations* 242–43). After his stint as a teacher, Vonnegut worked briefly in an advertising agency before opening the second Saab car dealership in the United States. In October of 1957 his father died, and, less than a year later, in 1958, Vonnegut's sister, Alice, would die of cancer, twenty-four hours after her husband's accidental death aboard a commuter train. Out of this family tragedy, Vonnegut's immediate family grew; Vonnegut and his wife Jane adopted Alice's three oldest children.[4] The painfully random events surrounding his sister's and brother-in-law's deaths undoubtedly helped solidify many of Vonnegut's convictions concerning the nature of the universe. From his personal pain and the immediate financial needs of caring for a family that now included six children, Vonnegut spun a tale of science fiction angst to an editor he happened to bump into at a dinner party. The editor inquired if Vonnegut was planning on writing another novel, and, according to Vonnegut, who had no idea for a new book but was not inclined to pass by such a fortuitous opportunity, he proceeded to tell the unsuspecting editor the story of *The Sirens of Titan* amidst the leisurely conversation of the dinner party (Allen, *Conversations* 35). Vonnegut often speaks fondly about the writing of his second novel. The book, unlike so much of the author's other writing, flowed freely, requiring little revision. As Vonnegut explains, "*The Sirens* was a case of automatic writing, almost. That wasn't a bashing book because I just started and I wrote it" (Allen, *Conversations* 158); elsewhere, he suggests that his warm, maternal feelings toward this work are a result of its delivery by "natural childbirth" (Allen, *Conversations* 35).

In *Understanding Kurt Vonnegut*, Allen argues that because of the lengthy duration between novels and Vonnegut's continued success with the short story form, the end result of his second novel is a work that "lacks a coherent center" (35). Going so far as to suggest that the novel's casual origin betrays its weakness, Allen characterizes it as thematically diffuse, inconsistent in terms of characterization and tone, and prone to wandering from subject to subject (35–36). On the contrary, I contend that Vonnegut's years of apprenticeship writing short stories for an audience that demanded clarity and orderly plot progression helped to hone his narrative skills, and the personal tragedy he experienced in the year before the composition of *The Sirens of Titan* seemingly generated a natural and coherent center for the book. Indeed, when *The Sirens of Titan* appeared in 1959, it represented the work of an author contemplating such weighty issues as divine providence and the nature of existence, issues that had been abruptly and tragically placed before the author. The form Vonnegut employed to examine such issues, however, was highly unconventional. Vonnegut chose the genre of science fiction, a genre that to this day does not often receive serious consideration from critics or scholars, in order to skewer the philosophical vanity that might somehow attempt to explain away the death of his sister and her husband. Most critics, perhaps because of the book's release as a paperback original, treated the work as one more inconsequential piece of science fiction trash in the world of dime store novels. Interestingly, the marketing of Vonnegut's work with a lurid cover displaying scantily clad women helped develop a devoted readership, a literate subculture that eventually led critics to give his fiction scholarly, albeit belated, attention. Today as we weigh Vonnegut's second novel, our consideration should be given not only to Vonnegut's themes, but also to his unique use of the science fiction form.

If we accept Frederick Buechner's assertion that art frames certain moments in life and heightens such moments, enabling us to better understand our human condition, then the moment that Vonnegut frames in *The Sirens of Titan* focuses on the cosmological education of one man: Malachi Constant. The education of Malachi Constant is arguably Vonnegut's attempt to educate humanity. Such an education works against humanity's fixation with meaning and order in a universe that Vonnegut conceives of as random and purposeless. While Vonnegut does attack the notion of an orderly universe, his most scathing critique is saved for individuals like Constant, who believe "somebody up there likes me." The entire book revolves around the misadventures of Constant; it is his wanderings across the universe, from Mars to Mercury to Titan and finally to Indianapolis, that exemplify Vonnegut's witty and moralistic punch line. Appropriately, Malachi's name actually means "constant messenger," and within the novel's frame, he consistently reinforces Vonnegut's claim that, indeed, there is no deity above showing favoritism toward one group of people while insuring the misfortune of another group of people.

While *Player Piano* works on the fringes of the science fiction genre, merely veiling Vonnegut's real-life experience with General Electric, *The Sirens of Titan* seems to embrace its every convention. *Sirens* is replete with time travel, space travel, alien creatures, devastating attacks from outer space, and beautiful women. But to conclude that Vonnegut writes straight science fiction is to make the same mistake as the publishing industry of 1959. In a fashion similar to that of Ray Bradbury—a writer of science fiction whom Vonnegut admires—Vonnegut's science fiction actually has little believable science in it. In fact when we compare the work of Bradbury or Vonnegut to that of Robert Heinlein or Arthur C. Clarke, we discover that Bradbury's and Vonnegut's work is woefully incomplete; their vision of the future has not worn well. Quite likely, such a comparison to Heinlein and Clarke would not disturb Bradbury or Vonnegut. Unlike other writers of science fiction, Bradbury and Vonnegut have shown little concern for the technology their stories entail: their space ships, rusted and in disrepair from lack of use, now seem fit only for low budget B-movies, while their reveries of the future have all but been surpassed by the real advances of a culture preoccupied with the possibilities of technological production. It is their writing, however, that endures. Because they focus on what is most human in their stories, the sweeping changes in technology have done nothing to tarnish their work. Although Bradbury and Vonnegut differ dramatically in their vision and use of science fiction, it is their humanity that continues to illuminate our path through the twenty-first century. For Bradbury, the human rests firmly in the individual hearts and minds of his characters; his is a world of microcosm. Vonnegut on the other hand, while still concerned with humanity, approaches his work macrocosmically; he consistently struggles with the overarching philosophical questions of human existence. Therefore, although *The Sirens of Titan* appears to embrace the generic conventions of science fiction, it actually undercuts those very conventions in order to support its theme of humanity's vanity and greed.

In *Structuring the Void*, Klinkowitz suggests that Vonnegut's use of science fiction follows the same satirical pattern exhibited in his other work, a pattern motivated by his distrust of science. Klinkowitz differentiates, however, between uncritical science fiction, practiced by such writers as Heinlein, and critical science fiction, practiced by the likes of Vonnegut:

> On the one hand, the science fiction mentality—equipped as it is with a mentality that believes any and all problems can be solved by the miracle of science—risks engendering an attitude

that the earth is just a throwaway planet, easily discardable when used up as we move on to greener fields across the universe. On the other hand, this same attitude encourages an intellectual solipsism that regards human life on earth as the absolute center of all meaning, a narrative perspective from which all other creation is to be evaluated and judged. (43)

The mentality represented by uncritical science fiction is anathema to Vonnegut. Vonnegut, however, does not respond to such literature with violence or verbal assaults; instead he lampoons the conventions embraced so fervently by science fiction aficionados. A fine example of such burlesque involves the Tralfamadorians, who we discover by novel's end have manipulated all of human history to convey simple messages concerning a repair part for a Tralfamadorian's broken-down spacecraft. Salo, Malachi's Tralfamadorian companion on Titan, explains that Stonehenge is simply the Tralfamadorian message that the "replacement part is being rushed with all possible speed"; that the Great Wall of China means, "Be patient. We haven't forgotten about you"; and that the Moscow Kremlin encouragingly states, "You will be on your way before you know it" (271).

Where other writers may have described alien life, such as the Tralfamadorians, in pseudoscientific discourse designed to impress the reader with their potential to wreak havoc or perpetuate peace, Vonnegut, using what he refers to as slapstick humor, tells the reader that Tralfamadorians look a great deal like plumber's helpers. With the use of such a mundane object as a plumber's helper to represent alien life and the notion that some of humanity's most brilliant achievements were merely practical messages for an alien with vehicle trouble, Vonnegut not only destroys the idea of some superior life-form inhabiting an unknown region of the universe, he also minimizes the achievements of human history. Such moralizing about the true importance of human life in relation to the universe remains a consistent theme throughout Vonnegut's career, perhaps culminating most darkly in *Galápagos*. What makes this theme so engaging in Vonnegut's fiction, however, is the tension between his acerbically witty humbling of humanity and his insistence that to love and serve humanity is our highest calling. The origin of the Tralfamadorian race reflects the nature of this tension. Salo explains to Malachi that the exact origin of Tralfamadorians is unknown; the current state of reproduction among the Tralfamadorians consists of the manufacturing of one another. Among the Tralfamadorians, however, there is a legend of a time when there were creatures unlike machines:

> They weren't dependable. They weren't efficient. They weren't predictable. They weren't durable. And these poor creatures were obsessed by the idea that everything that existed had to have a purpose, and that some purposes were higher than others.
>
> These creatures spent most of their time trying to find out what their purpose was. And every time they found out what seemed to be a purpose of themselves, the purpose seemed so low that the creatures were filled with disgust and shame.
>
> And, rather than serve such a low purpose, the creatures would make a machine to serve it. This left the creatures free to serve higher purposes. But whenever they found a higher purpose, the purpose still wasn't high enough.
>
> So machines were made to serve higher purposes, too. And the machines did everything so expertly that they were finally given the job of finding out what the highest purpose of the creatures could be.
>
> The machines reported in all honesty that the creatures couldn't really be said to have any purpose at all. The creatures thereupon began slaying each other, because they hated purposeless things above all else.
>
> And they discovered that they weren't even very good at slaying.
>
> So they turned that job over to the machines, too. And the machines finished up the job in less time than it takes to say, "Tralfamadore." (274–75)

I quote this passage in full because of its centrality to the discussion of moral tension in Vonnegut's work. Of particular note is the style in which Vonnegut chooses to tell his tale. Rather than attempt to deal with the nature of human history in dialogue, Vonnegut places his philosophical and historical interpretation of our past in a religious myth delivered by a machine in monologue. By using the mythic form, Vonnegut finds a discourse appropriate to his admonitions, and by using a machine, he gains a distanced objectivity that may allow the reader more freedom to mull over this pointed and practical history lesson.

By using Tralfamadorian history to retell our own history, Vonnegut turns uncritical science fiction on its ear. Instead of telling a story of some distant planet where life is far more appealing than our own, Vonnegut allows an alien machine to show us that life remains pretty much the same all over. *The Sirens of Titan* offers no escape to other worlds of flight and fancy—the desired effect of many science fiction novels; rather, it turns the lens back toward the twentieth century, to a planet called Earth, inhabited by unusual creatures who have christened themselves "humans." A master of clarity, Vonnegut assures us that, of course, we are the very same creatures who consistently look for meaning in all we do, who hate purposelessness, and who have developed machines that kill far more efficiently than we can on our own. Such characteristics, he suggests, lead only to destruction. But Vonnegut rallies against such destruction, against the pervasive assumption that everything we do need be charged with meaning, that purposelessness is to be rued. His fight against these grand narratives, however, implies that we are in some way worth saving. The paradoxical nature of Vonnegut's moral philosophy lies in his efforts to disrupt our vain and pretentious self-serving actions, while never slipping into a misanthropic reverie. Despite his dark and mordant depiction of humanity, he relentlessly and tirelessly crusades for the human race.

Of course, Malachi Constant is not allowed to learn Vonnegut's lesson quickly; he is a slow study when it comes to universal lessons. Vonnegut, without subtlety, makes sure the reader understands that Malachi is a Jonah figure; in fact, Malachi uses the name Jonah Rowley when he visits Rumfoord's estate, preparing the reader for his anxious flight from Rumfoord's prophecy. Stanley Schatt claims that "By being forced to journey in *The Whale* and undergo almost unbearable torments, the passive Malachi, like Jonah, loses all feelings of selfishness and callousness toward his fellow man" (32). As Jonah, Malachi becomes the focal point for Vonnegut's moral discourse. Unlike Allen, who argues that Rumfoord is the intellectual hero of the novel because he "sees through all the fake programs limiting the understanding of others and breaks through to pure existential freedom" (*Understanding* 41), I suggest that Rumfoord is only one more characterization of humanity's struggle for power, and ultimately Vonnegut will not reward him. Although Rumfoord is instrumental in transforming an entire culture by staging a war between Mars and Earth and establishing the Church of God the Utterly Indifferent, by using Malachi he violates the sanctity of the individual. Rumfoord, who Vonnegut explains is based on Franklin Delano Roosevelt, may wish to create a better world, but in perpetrating his scheme he crosses the line between his own humanity and the inhumane urge to play God. In the end, his actions appear to be no better than those of any other dictator attempting to control the course of human life. We cannot forget that it is Rumfoord's grand scheme that calls for Malachi to strangle his best friend and that it is Rumfoord who plans for thousands of innocent people to be lobotomized and trained for the army of Mars in order that they may be sent to their deaths in a suicide attack on Earth. Rumfoord shows no mercy toward anyone in the novel. Therefore, while I agree in part with Allen's characterization of Rumfoord as the intellectual hero of the novel—after all, he delivers speech after speech describing the nature of the universe—I suggest Rumfoord experiences no freedom, existential or otherwise. In fact, Rumfoord's existence consists of imprisonment; he is a victim of the chrono-synclastic infundibulum, appearing on Earth every fifty-nine days whether he wishes to or not. By novel's end, Vonnegut sends Rumfoord across the universe in a cocoon of green energy, permanently separating him from his faithful dog, Kazak, without giving him the opportunity to discover the Tralfamadorian message that Salo carries or to understand the beauty of human compassion and love.

The many lessons to be learned from Rumfoord are integral to Malachi's education.[5] But, in the end, it is Malachi who discovers the purpose of human life. We must remember that the story of *The Sirens of Titan* issues forth from some point in the future, years after the Second World War and the Third Great Depression, a future where people explore an "inwardness" that is "the beginning of goodness and wisdom" (8). Therefore, Malachi's wanderings across the universe, according to the narrator, represent "empty heroics, low comedy, and pointless death" (8). From the outset, Vonnegut prepares the reader for the moral nature of his novel, and as we read *The Sirens of Titan*, we discover that, as promised, there are empty heroics, low comedy, and pointless death. Appropriate to the telling of a moral tale, however, after following Malachi's cosmological journey, we are rewarded with Malachi's turn inward, "the beginning of goodness and wisdom."

Malachi's turn inward results from his relationship with Beatrice, his human mate on Titan. Because of his long exile with Beatrice, who during the course of the story is transformed from a beautiful and vain young woman to a scarred and disfigured elderly one, Malachi comes to understand his cosmic lesson. Beatrice's transformation from a vain creature of supreme physical beauty to a humble creature of spiritual beauty mirrors Malachi's own transformation, and, like Malachi, she works against Rumfoord's idea that the only purpose for human life is to deliver a Tralfamadorian repair part by writing a book entitled *The True Purpose of Life in the Solar System*.

Soon after the death of Beatrice, Malachi tells Salo that an earthling year before her death, they discovered "that a purpose of human life, no matter who is controlling it, is to love whoever is around to be loved" (313). Simple, aphoristic, and sentimental, Malachi's lesson, nonetheless, remains compelling. Because of the fantastical nature of the journey he has taken, a journey filled with the sorrows and joys only life holds, his conclusion resonates with meaning. Ironically, Malachi's education has required him to travel far beyond the confines of the United States, but it is to the heart of our country that Vonnegut returns him. Salo offers to drop Malachi off on his way home to Tralfamadore, but grows worried when Malachi insists that he be left in Indianapolis, Indiana. Malachi wishes to be left in Vonnegut's hometown for one simple reason, a reason that reinforces the ethical center of the book: "'Indianapolis, Indiana,' said Constant, 'is the first place in the United States of America where a white man was hanged for the murder of an Indian. The kind of people who'll hang a white man for murdering an Indian—' said Constant, 'that's the kind of people for me'" (314–15). After his moral education, the kind of people for Malachi are people who see all of humanity as equal, deserving compassion and consideration and love. Malachi no longer rests assured that he deserves Providential treatment, an attitude that served as the rationale for the heinous annihilation of so many peoples, Native Americans among them. Therefore, it is fitting that the last act described in the book is an act of compassion performed by an alien machine who looked very much like a plumber's helper. Salo hypnotizes Malachi when he leaves him on a park bench in Indianapolis, and as Malachi dies, snow drifting down over him, he imagines that his best friend, Stony Stevenson, flies down from the heavens in a spaceship in order to take him to paradise, where he will be joined by Beatrice. Much like Salo's vision, Vonnegut's vision, whether it is real or imagined, offers an epiphany wherein we may learn to care for one another, a vision of cosmological importance rooted in a simple Midwestern faith.

Mother Night and Cat's Cradle: Vonnegut's Descent into Darkness

Vonnegut's career has been described as a series of ebbs and flows. In *Sanity Plea*, Broer argues that these shifts ultimately represent Vonnegut's own creative schizophrenia, while Allen, in *Understanding Kurt Vonnegut*, claims that such shifts are inextricably bound to the formal success or failure of each work. Another way of looking at the ebbs and flows in Vonnegut's writing involves his vision of life and death, hope and despair. The uneasy play between Vonnegut's hopeful movement toward the light and his uncompromising chronicling of the dark represents the core of his artistic world. Never is his vision complete; no single work embraces fully a vision of hope or despair. Vonnegut's work symbolizes an interplay like that of the yin and yang in Taoist philosophy. For example, *Player Piano* ends with no clear resolution; although there is the fear that the same old nightmare may be recreated in Ilium, the fact that there are individuals like Paul Proteus intimates that we are not left without hope. *The Sirens of Titan*, on the other hand, ends with a literal movement toward the light as Malachi believes he is journeying to paradise, a most welcome ending to a novel flooded with the dark and horrific randomness of the universe. Vonnegut's subsequent two novels, however, journey further into darkness, toward death's alluring call, than any other work to date. Each novel offers the possibility of hope, but each ultimately works its way toward the threat of suicide. What exactly hastens this movement toward Mother Night, the dark embrace of oblivion that Howard W. Campbell Jr., contemplates and Bokonon writes of in his final sentence in *The Books of Bokonon*, is the matter of our existence. As I argued earlier, Vonnegut's work consistently wrestles with the nature of our existence. It asks repeatedly, Who or what controls the universe, and what is our purpose in being here? Such questions haunt him. In the oscillation between the yin and yang, however, we encounter a wide range of characters in the fiction, some who deal

well with the "not knowing" of existence and others whose
demands for assurance lead to self-annihilation.

Through the use of what some have called black humor, Vonnegut combats the despair that leads to self-annihilation.[6] In a
review of the hardcover reissue of *Mother Night* in 1966, Richard
Schickel claims that the novel is far from a capitulation to
despair; it "is on the contrary, a wonderful splash of bright, pri-
mary colors, an artful, zestful cartoon that lets us see despair
without forcing us to surrender to it. There is no self-pity at the
core of Vonnegut's work, only the purifying laughter of a man
who has survived that stage" (103). Vonnegut uses humor to face
what for many seems impossible to face: the lack of definitive
control over human existence. His humor entails the absurdity of
everyday events that constantly thwart our intentions to make
sense of the world, and, perhaps what makes Vonnegut the master of such humor is his ability to build absurdity upon absurdity,
story upon story, toward a thunderous punch line that in the end
appears to be an admonition to the reader not to journey down
the dark path of absolutism but, rather, to embrace the free play
of life in an attempt to help humanity. *Mother Night* presents a
fine example of what James Lundquist calls "compounded absurdity" (32). Through an intricate series of events, Howard Campbell Jr.'s, every aspiration is humiliatingly reversed. Campbell
exclaims, "The part of me that wanted to tell the truth got turned
into an expert liar! The lover in me got turned into a pornogra-
pher! The artist in me got turned into ugliness such as the world
has rarely seen before" (150). His failings are fodder for the Vonnegut lesson book. Our destiny rests in the hands of a universe
whose only consideration is material, and our vain attempts to
create narratives that suggest otherwise, as well as our blind faith
in the absolute truth of such narratives, will forever be thwarted.
At every turn, Campbell's belief in some essential truth leads to
his comic downfall. Campbell trusts that his work as a Nazi does
not represent his essential humanity; after all, the only reason he
spews forth such propaganda is to make him a more effective spy
for the United States. Campbell hopes that his love for Helga in
some way will make him immune to the ills of a country bent on
war and genocide; he fails to realize that we are all part of a complex system where our actions affect every member of the community, not simply a select few. The absurdity of his misplaced
trust concludes with the deaths of thousands of Jews at the hands

of people who, in part, have been encouraged to commit such heinous crimes by the speeches of Campbell; the love that Campbell hoped might isolate him from the tragedy of war ends with the death of Helga and the cuckolding of Campbell by Resi, Helga's sister, who poses as Helga in New York City years after the war. Campbell's problem is made most clear by Vonnegut in a poem written by Campbell:

> Here lies Howard Campbell's essence,
> Freed from his body's noisome nuisance.
> His body, empty, prowls the earth,
> Earning what a body's worth.
> If his body and his essence remain apart,
> Burn his body, but spare this, his heart. (96)

Campbell believes that his heart, or essence, remains innocent of the crimes his body commits, that appearance is not reality. *Mother Night*, by chronicling the war crimes of Campbell, makes us privy to Campbell's hard learned revelation: we are what we appear to be. This lesson, of course, is integral to Vonnegut as he dismantles those grand narratives of modernism based on the idea of essence, because it suggests that the narratives championed by postmodernism must be told carefully and with great consideration.

Just as in *Player Piano*, in *Mother Night* and *Cat's Cradle*, Vonnegut, by continuing to struggle against the narrative framework of American culture, establishes an ethical code that insists that because the only way we may know our world is through language, the narratives we choose to tell have no essential truth. But Vonnegut warns that even if there is no essential truth behind narratives, those narratives that we do choose to tell are crucial because they either contribute to our well-being or to our destruction whether they are true or not. Therefore, the darkness that enshrouds *Mother Night* and *Cat's Cradle* is a darkness that works against itself. When Vonnegut leads us into the darkness, showing us the despair of those who trust too fully in the essential truth of our culture's narratives, he hopes that we will not be lost to absolutism, but instead will see the light of relativity. Out of darkness, Vonnegut demystifies and decenters the grand narratives of America while beginning to offer inevitably provisional answers, the only kind there are to the questions of a postmodern condition. Although these novels do not formally exhibit the post-modernity of *Slaughterhouse-Five* and later novels, both do begin to play with the structures of narrative and chapter length. *Mother Night* subverts the spy novel, a traditionally modernist genre, in an attempt to expose the metanarratives of war and governmental operation, a theme or project that culminates in *Slaughterhouse-Five*. *Cat's Cradle*, on the other hand, begins to reveal Vonnegut's interest in playing with the conventions of the novel, as exhibited by its move away from conventional chapters; *Cat's Cradle* offers 127 such breaks while affording the reader a clear view of the novel's own constructedness, concluding with a final chapter entitled, "The End." Although in *Mother Night* Vonnegut avoids using chapters or other formal conventions to the same effect as *Cat's Cradle*, he does work within a genre of unusual popular appeal—Ian Fleming was certainly having great success at the time with James Bond—a genre that traditionally reifies the master narrative of a country's position, a position that is unquestioningly ordained by some truth, a manifest destiny. The formula for such books revolves around harrowing acts perpetrated by the spy that may under other circumstances be deemed morally questionable, but in the fictional context are always justified by the country's grand narrative. The first readers of *Mother Night* must have been shocked to read a spy novel in which the actions of the protagonist, by never being clearly defined, leave the reader to question the nature of good and evil, right and wrong.

Vonnegut uses the spy genre in *Mother Night* to subvert not only the function of the genre itself, but also the grand narrative of American supremacy in matters of war and peace. Howard Campbell, an American spy in Nazi Germany, is an incredibly successful propagandist for the Nazi regime. Vonnegut's repeated questioning of our ability to know or apprehend truth begins at the outset in an editor's note, written by the editor of *Mother Night*, none other than Kurt Vonnegut Jr. himself. The editor claims that the text before the reader is the American edition of the confessions of Campbell and then launches into a muddled paragraph on the nature of lying, explaining that "lies told for the sake of artistic effect—in the theater, for instance, and in Campbell's confessions, perhaps—can be, in a higher sense, the most beguiling forms of truth" (ix). Certainly the readers of the original paperback release—readers who were not afforded the luxury of Vonnegut's introduction to the 1966 hardback reissue—were

confronted with the task of deciphering the "truth" of Vonnegut's
position as editor and the likelihood that Campbell had ever
existed as a "real" person. *Mother Night*, as the title might indi-
cate, is one of Vonnegut's darkest works, and one in which he
examines the enduring issue of appearance versus reality, only to
conclude that there is no difference between "pretending" and
"being," a lesson Campbell learns too late and one that ends with
his suicide. Clinton S. Burhans claims that the novel is Vonnegut's
argument "that the reality within man is no essential self, no inde-
pendent soul unconditioned and untouched by his behavior. . . .
We are, that is, what we do, not what we say; what we do at any
particular time establishes what we are" (179). What is at stake in
the argument of "being" and "doing" is essence. If there is some
essence, some core of existence that goes beyond our constructed
worlds, then Campbell's actions may be predicated on some center of good or evil, a center that permits harmful acts to be committed in the name of good, in the name of justice, in the name of
the United States. But Vonnegut dismisses such a world. As he says
in the introduction to the hardcover reissue of the novel written in
1966 while he taught in Iowa City, "We are what we pretend to
be, so we must be careful about what we pretend to be" (v). Vonnegut's own comments on the moral to *Mother Night* begin to
offer a provisional answer to the postmodern condition. In a
decentered world, we are fictions, constructing our own realities
and truths, so we must be careful what we construct. It would
appear that Vonnegut reasons along the same lines as Jean Baudrillard, who explains, "Moralists about war, champions of war's
exalted values should not be greatly upset: a war is not any the
less heinous for being a mere simulacrum—flesh suffers just the
same, and the dead excombatants count as much there as in other
wars" (371). Whether Campbell's propaganda is merely a pose, a
fiction constructed to hide his identity as an American spy,
remains insignificant; the heinous acts that he helps lead the German people to commit in the name of Nazism are quite real; the
deaths of the millions of Jews cannot be erased with language.
Grand narratives, the fictions we construct, even if their constructedness is exposed, still do as much harm as those that are
hidden, and for that reason Vonnegut urges us to choose those
narratives that are "harmless."

Foma, or harmless untruths, are the basis for *Cat's Cradle*, a
novel that works against the grand narrative that may be most

central to American culture: religion. The novel, like *Mother Night*, begins with a disclaimer of sorts: "Nothing in this book is true. 'Live by the foma that make you brave and kind and healthy and happy.'" The second half of this passage is taken from *The Books of Bokonon*, the religious text that takes the place of the Christian Bible in the novel, and points more clearly to Vonnegut's provisional answer to the postmodern condition, to what Gayatri Spivak, in remarks given at the Center for the Humanities at Wesleyan University in the spring of 1985, calls an "operational essentialism, a false ontology" (qtd. in Butler 325). Religion, more specifically Christianity, may be argued to be the single most significant narrative that undergirds the structure of American culture; it poses as the center for truth, for referentiality, in both overt and covert ways. While Christianity's sphere of influence has diminished in intellectual communities, it undoubtedly remains the foundation for the premodern and modern conception of language and essence. This connection between language and essence is demonstrated most dramatically in the Christian Bible when the author of the New Testament book of John proclaims: "In the beginning was the Word, and the Word was with God, and the Word was God. . . . And the Word became flesh, and dwelt among us, and we beheld His glory, glory as of the only begotten from the Father, full of grace and truth" (John 1:1). The grounding of presence in language clearly follows from a conception of God as the Word, a God who spoke the universe into existence. Our trust in language and the narratives we create out of language has developed over thousands of years, and the philosophical movement of deconstruction has hardly made a dent in the collective psyche of the West, including America. Even in intellectual circles, Derridean ideas of language have met serious resistance. It appears that our culture largely continues to live with the unspoken understanding that essence and language are indelibly linked, that work and play and value systems are natural products of reality and not the product of narrative structures. In his own matchless way, Vonnegut works persistently to challenge how we perceive reality. Whether he is pioneering the metafictional techniques that made his work the focus of postmodern studies by such critics as Brian McHale or Linda Hutcheon or constructing intricate jokes out of narrative threads ultimately leading to grim punch lines, his efforts remain centered on the way we conceive of, and, hence, perceive reality.

Like Malachi Constant in *The Sirens of Titan*, the narrator of *Cat's Cradle* tells the reader to call him Jonah, a clear allusion to Melville's Ishmael, another character in American literature whose quest for a centered truth falls short.[7] The figure of Jonah fits perfectly his creator's purposes: It is the recalcitrant nature of Jonah that represents our own reluctance to see beyond the surface to the constructed narratives supporting what we call reality. Vonnegut's Jonah mirrors our own stubborn refusal to admit that the only meaning in the universe is the meaning we create for ourselves. In fact, it may be argued that Vonnegut furthers the transcendental and romantic tradition of Emerson and Melville in his disdain for static, definitive meaning; for Vonnegut, as for Emerson and Melville, there can never be singular truth, only the shifting, changing, and developing truths that we discover in searching the self. Not surprisingly, Jonah, like most narrators in Vonnegut's fiction, immediately divulges the purpose for the telling of his tale, a purpose bound by the façade of factuality and eventually undermined by Bokononism:

> When I was a much younger man, I began to collect material for a book to be called *The Day the World Ended*.
> The book was to be factual.
> The book was to be an account of what important Americans had done on the day when the first atomic bomb was dropped on Hiroshima, Japan.
> It was to be a Christian book. I was a Christian then.
> I am a Bokononist now. (11)

Less than half a page into the novel, Vonnegut gives us a narrator who, when he was much younger, believed in the grand narrative of Christianity and in its ability to undergird the writing of a "factual" book that could somehow explain the atrocity of the first atomic bomb. The book our narrator actually writes is a history of the Hoenikker family and Bokononism, a book that portrays the ignorant sinfulness of science, humanity's need for love, and the usefulness of religion. Jonah discovers, through his bizarre descent into the lives of the Hoenikker family and later into the religion of Bokononism, that truth is constructed and relative. Ironically, Jonah does indeed write a book about the end of the world: *Cat's Cradle* concludes with what appears to be the certain demise of the human race.

The main action of the novel, however, deals with Jonah's discovery of Bokononism, a religion that paradoxically offers a narrative for living without establishing a metanarrative; it is the first formal example of petite histoire in Vonnegut's fiction. *Mother Night* establishes that we do indeed construct our own reality in our pretending to be a spy or a lover or a nation, but *Cat's Cradle* goes one step further and demonstrates how life can be "based" on a provisional narrative, on an ever-changing petite histoire, without claiming a centered or essential presence. When the narrator asks to see a copy of *The Books of Bokonon*, he is told that copies are hard to come by: "They aren't printed. They're made by hand. And, of course, there is no such thing as a completed copy, since Bokonon is adding things every day" (124). Bokononists must always be aware that because the basis for their living is mere fabrication, any flirtation with absolutism would be absurd. Klinkowitz asserts that since Bokononism is a faith of "self-apparent pretense and artifice," for such "artifice to succeed it must always maintain its identity as arbitrary convention and never succumb to temptations of absolute truth" (*Structuring* 47). The artificial nature of which Klinkowitz speaks presents the ideal conditions for postmodernity's small narratives. Bokononism functions solely with small narratives and embraces the local over the universal. Such narratives, as Pauline Marie Rosenau explains, substitute for theory and truth those community-based narratives that "focus on the local, assert neither truth nor totalizing theory, and propose no broad theoretical generalizations or ultimate truths. They are offered as only one interpretation among many" (84). The grand narrative of Christianity is found in the Bible, complete with a beginning and an end, an essential and totalizing truth; the petite histoire of Bokononism is found in its own books, incomplete, fragmented, without a clear beginning or end. Still, as Mary Sue Schriber argues, foma have a redemptive social value: "They force us to see and simultaneously to laugh at limitations, preventing us from believing that truth can be known, defending us from an inhuman absolutism that the narrator equates with insanity" (288). Absolutism, the absurd belief that one's own ideas are unerringly correct, that one's actions may be driven by an essential good or purity, leads to the dark conclusion of *Cat's Cradle*.

What makes *Cat's Cradle* such an engaging novel, however, is the human story behind our desire for absolutism. While Vonnegut ridicules science in the person of Dr. Hoenikker for its ignorant belief that somehow what it deals with is essential truth, free from any other influence, he counters with a positive depiction of science in the person of Dr. von Koenigswald, who is most concerned with bettering the human condition. Through his interviews with family members and colleagues, Jonah slowly puts together a portrait of Hoenikker as a man oblivious of the danger his own mind holds, of the purposes to which his discoveries may be put. In a letter from Dr. Hoenikker's son, Newton, we learn what Dr. Hoenikker says after the testing of his new invention, the atomic bomb: "After the thing went off, after it was a sure thing that America could wipe out a city with just one bomb, a scientist turned to Father and said, 'Science has now known sin.' And do you know what Father said? He said, 'What is sin?'" (21). Hoenikker represents Vonnegut's greatest fears: a man who has a mind so brilliant that he can find the means to destroy the world, but who has no conception of right or wrong, of moral value. On the other hand, Dr. von Koenigswald, who appears much later in the novel on San Lorenzo, explains ironically that "I am a very bad scientist. I will do anything to make a human being feel better, even if it's unscientific" (148). Koenigswald, while still a man of science—he admits to Jonah that the one idea of Bokononism he agrees with is that all religions are nothing but lies—is willing to sacrifice his scientific ideology in order "to make a human being feel better." This is the man of science whom Vonnegut embraces, a figure not unlike Vonnegut's brother, Bernard, or even Vonnegut himself.

Indeed, although he consistently critiques the world of science, Vonnegut remains a man of science. We must not forget that *Cat's Cradle* served as his thesis when the University of Chicago awarded him a master's degree in anthropology in 1971. In fact, *Cat's Cradle* incorporates many of the ideas Vonnegut was first introduced to when he began his study at the University of Chicago in 1945.[8] While his original thesis, "Fluctuations Between Good and Evil in Simple Tales," was not accepted in 1947, the ideas of Dr. Robert Redfield concerning the needs of humans and the notion of cultural relativity continued to surface in Vonnegut's work. Jerome Klinkowitz explains in *Structuring the Void* that Vonnegut's anthropological training "convinced him that reality was something arbitrary and impermanent, since the basic facts of life could be changed by circumstances of birth or by the whims of national economics even after one was half-grown" (37). Such an anthropological lesson is especially poignant for Vonnegut

because of his German ancestry. As he explains in the 1966 introduction to *Mother Night*, "If I'd been born in Germany, I suppose
I would have *been* a Nazi, bopping Jews and gypsies and Poles
around, leaving boots sticking out of snowbanks, warming myself
with my secretly virtuous insides. So it goes" (vii). Vonnegut's sar-
donic comment about "secretly virtuous insides" clearly reflects
his disdain for any argument that suggests an essential goodness
within humanity. Seemingly, we are the products of the narratives
we choose to tell, the narratives our communities embrace as
truth. That Nazi Germany chose atrocious narratives on which to
build its communities offers a lesson Vonnegut does not want anyone soon to forget.

In a moment of versified levity, Vonnegut pokes fun at our collective situation, at our need to tell our stories:

> We do,
> Doodley do, doodley do, doodley do,
> What we must,
> Muddily must, muddily must, muddily must;
> Muddily do,
> Muddily do, Muddily do, muddily do,
> Until we bust,
> Bodily bust, bodily bust, bodily bust.
> (*Wampeters* xxiv)

Vonnegut's verse advances the idea that we tell our stories in an
attempt to represent our experiences and ultimately to transform
those experiences, to "muddily do" until we "bodily bust." Our
stories are, however, the only tools we possess for improving the
human condition; narratives create community, and community,
in turn, establishes a setting in which work may be done. For Vonnegut, communities based on the family structure may be the most
hopeful response the postmodern horizon holds.[9] During the time
he studied anthropology at the University of Chicago, Vonnegut
was introduced to the work of Redfield, including his lengthy discourse on folk societies. Redfield's theory suggests that all human
beings, for physical and emotional well-being, need to belong to
extended families, localized communities. But such communities
are not as plentiful as one might think. As Vonnegut remarks: "it
is curious that such communities should be so rare, since human
beings are genetically such gregarious creatures. They need plenty

of like-minded friends and relatives almost as much as they need B-complex vitamins and a heartfelt moral code" (*Palm Sunday* 204). These folk societies, a topic that comes up repeatedly in the interviews, essays, and speeches of Vonnegut, are the structures, admittedly built on some communal narrative, from which Vonnegut argues for a postmodern humanism. Such communities, according to Vonnegut, provide people with a shared moral code and companionship, a created purpose for existence. Although folk societies offer hope for living in a postmodern world, such a response does not come without the possibility for harm. In *Fates Worse Than Death*, he acknowledges the danger implicit in folk societies: "The trouble begins when a person suffering from FSD (Folk Society Deficiency) stops thinking, in order to become a member of an artificial extended family which happens to be crazy. The homicidal 'family' of Charles Manson springs to mind. Or what about the cult of the Reverend Jim Jones in Guyana, whose members on his advice ('Tonight you will be with me in Paradise') fed the kids Kool-Aid laced with cyanide and then drank it themselves" (126).

Finally, the dark conclusion of *Cat's Cradle* may be attributed to the lack of familial love and acceptance experienced by the Hoenikker children. Felix Hoenikker himself does not experience what Vonnegut argues is as necessary for human survival as "B-complex vitamins and a heartfelt moral code." As a father and husband, he is absent, entirely detached from human life, and his final legacy to his children is a substance that can effectively end all human life. Marvin Breed, the scientist in the novel who supervises Hoenikker's projects, says of him, "Sometimes I wonder if he wasn't born dead. I never met a man who was less interested in the living. Sometimes I think that's the trouble with the world: too many people in high places who are stone-cold dead" (53). And such people in high places are, of course, the very people who have the most power to construct narratives of hope or despair. Out of Hoenikker's own life and death, his children come forth looking for family, for love, and with ice-nine they attempt to buy what cannot be bought. Angela's marriage to Harrison C. Conners, the president of Fabri-Tek in Indianapolis, Newton's marriage to Zinka, the Soviet spy, and Franklin's position as Major General and Minister of Science and Progress in the Republic of San Lorenzo, are all pitiful shams. In each case the Hoenikker children are used only for the precious ice-nine, and any dreams they may have had for the love they so dearly needed are swallowed up by a vast, frozen landscape.

Clearly, Vonnegut wishes families or folk societies existed in great quantities and worked with great success. The reality remains that they do not, and such a reality tenders only a journey into night, an ironic and brutally absurd dance with ice-nine. As the Hoenikker children discover, what we need most in life can never be bought; it must be created out of our own stories, stories that Vonnegut certainly hopes we learn to tell more carefully. Out of the icy dark of *Cat's Cradle*, however, we will find Vonnegut's own ascent into the heartland where Eliot Rosewater of Rosewater County, Indiana, attempts to establish a profound humanism in this new age. As John R. May argues in "Vonnegut's Humor and the Limits of Hope," "one still feels certain that Vonnegut, like the Bokononists, holds at least one thing sacred and that is man" (129).

God Bless You, Mr. Rosewater: Vonnegut's Gospel of Hope

May's conviction that Vonnegut holds at least one thing sacred is supported in compelling fashion by Vonnegut's subsequent novel, *God Bless You, Mr. Rosewater*. The novel appears to reflect Vonnegut's wish for a more hopeful future, one devoted to humanity, albeit in a nonsensical fashion. *God Bless You, Mr. Rosewater* gently and humorously carries the reader along on an ocean of uncritical love, offering an example of human kindness from an obese alcoholic who is fond of playing with his pubic hair. Rosewater, Indiana, decimated physically and spiritually, becomes the center for Eliot Rosewater's daring social experiment: how to love people who have no use, a nagging conundrum for Vonnegut since his first novel. Before the unprecedented critical and popular explosion of Vonnegut's writing in the conflagration of Dresden, he returned in his fiction to Indiana, not far from his childhood home, to explore the possibilities of hope. Without such a journey toward the light, his descent into the darkness of the slaughterhouse, into the horrifying landscape of burnt-out buildings and charred corpses may never have reached fruition. The question addressed in *God Bless You, Mr. Rosewater* is strikingly similar to that in *The Sirens of Titan*: What is the purpose of humanity? And just as Malachi Constant must wander the universe before finding an answer to this most difficult question, Eliot Rosewater also must travel across the United States before settling down in Rosewater, Indiana, where he comes to the realization that "people can use all the uncritical love they can get" (186). On the one hand, in *Player Piano* and *The Sirens of Titan* Vonnegut struggles with American culture, its increasing mechanization and its disparaging treatment of the individual who is slowly made obsolete not only by machines, but also by the practices of fellow humans. This struggle, however, remains distanced to some degree because of the conventions of science fiction. On the other hand, *God Bless You, Mr. Rosewater*, like *Mother Night*, is firmly situated in the twentieth century and marks Vonnegut's growing devotion to realism, a mode that will carry his work to its greatest success in the 1980s. Because of his turn to realism, his brutal attack on an American culture willing to sacrifice what is most human is heightened. There is no mistaking the author's intent. Unlike *Player Piano*, where the reader is forced to put the pieces together in order to discern that the futuristic town of Ilium and its complex of factories represents Vonnegut's own experience with General Electric, *God Bless You, Mr. Rosewater* uses a more realistic mode of fiction in order to depict the inherent evils in American culture. There is no mistaking Rosewater, Indiana, for some fabled, futuristic town; it clearly represents America in microcosm. Rosewater, Indiana, like America, has been laid waste by greed, by those who agree with the notion that made the Rosewaters so fabulously wealthy: "Grab much too much, or you'll get nothing at all" (*God Bless* 13).

Arguably the focus of Vonnegut's attack on American culture is money. He begins the novel with a direct statement: "A sum of money is a leading character in this tale about people, just as a sum of honey might properly be a leading character in a tale about bees" (7). Klinkowitz argues that Vonnegut's preoccupation with money in this novel relates to his own financial difficulties; the short story market that for a time was financially lucrative had all but vanished, and Vonnegut's novels had become mired in the paperback industry, earning little income (*Kurt Vonnegut* 58). While this autobiographical note surely gives some insight into what motivated such a visceral and staggering assault on the economic and social system of America, it fails to acknowledge that Vonnegut had already been preoccupied with the kinds of technological and economic progress that make humans obsolete. Moreover, the issue of money, as Vonnegut suggests, is merely a practical matter: as bees are drawn to honey, so are humans to money. The real crux of the tale is the treatment of humans; money happens to be a leading cause for the mistreatment of others, not the root of all evil. Ultimately, Vonnegut is not attacking the American dream as propounded by our constitutional ideals; rather, he is attacking the perverse and dramatic transformation of those ideals.

Very early in the novel Vonnegut establishes the ethical plumb line in a letter written by Eliot that is to be delivered to the next president of the Rosewater Foundation upon Eliot's death. In the letter Eliot briefly outlines his family's history and the unscrupulous practices that enabled them to amass their fortune, concluding that his ancestors are largely responsible for the current state of affairs:

> Thus did a handful of rapacious citizens come to control all that was worth controlling in America. Thus was the savage and stupid and entirely inappropriate and unnecessary and humorless American class system created. Honest, industrious, peaceful citizens were classed as blood suckers, if they asked to be paid a living wage. And they saw that praise was reserved henceforth for those who devised means of getting paid enormously for committing crimes against which no laws had beenpassed. Thus the American dream turned belly up, turned green, bobbed to the scummy surface of cupidity unlimited, filled with gas, went bang in the noonday sun. (12–13)

The history of cupidity, of course, is not America's alone, but Eliot laments that the United States of America, "which was meant to be a Utopia for all," has "gone bust." Some might argue that Eliot's diatribe against a culture that forsakes the welfare of humanity for selfish gain does not represent Vonnegut's ethical ideology; such an argument fails, however, in the face of Vonnegut's own comments. In an interview in 1973, Vonnegut suggested that the McGovern campaign use the following speech to defeat Nixon, a political defeat Vonnegut would have cheered:

> You're not happy, are you? Nobody in this country is happy but the rich people. Something is wrong. I'll tell you what's wrong:

We're lonesome! We're being kept apart from our neighbors. Why? Because the rich people can go on taking our money away if we don't hang together. They can go on taking our power away. They want us lonesome; they want us huddled in our houses with just our wives and kids, watching television, because they can manipulate us then. They can make us buy anything, they can make us vote anyway they want. How did Americans beat the Great Depression? We banded together. In those days, members of unions called each other "brother" and "sister" and they meant it. We're going to bring that spirit back. (Allen, *Conversations* 102–03)

The spirit of family, of caring for those with less, continues to build in intensity throughout Vonnegut's work, and the very campaign slogan he offers to the McGovern campaign—Lonesome no more!—eventually becomes the campaign slogan for the protagonist of *Slapstick*. Vonnegut wishes not so much to defeat the wealthy as, rather, to defeat the wrongful practices of the wealthy. Indeed, *God Bless You, Mr. Rosewater*, in some respects, may be seen as an instruction manual for the rich. Eliot is a virtuous model of philanthropy; he recognizes what we need most as humans and attempts to use his monetary resources to help alleviate the pain and suffering of others.

The story of how Eliot becomes a virtuous model, in spite of his ghastly physical appearance and unsavory habits, generates tension between the superficial and the ideal, between appearance and reality. In order to expose the insanity of our mistreatment of one another and the sanity of Eliot's response to such mistreatment, Vonnegut uses the story of Hamlet.[10] Eliot, as a modern-day Hamlet, plays the role to perfection, vacillating between madness and sanity. Vonnegut forces the reader to analyze Eliot's actions: Is he deranged for setting up shop in Rosewater and attending to the needs of the less fortunate, or is it the world that has gone mad in neglecting the poor? Certainly, by novel's end we are to believe that there is method in Eliot's madness, that, indeed, Eliot does know a hawk from a handsaw. The first evidence of Eliot's identification with Hamlet occurs when he delivers a speech to a group of science fiction writers attending a convention in Milford, Pennsylvania. Eliot boozily proclaims that his favorite science fiction writer, Kilgore Trout, will some day be the only man remembered from our time for such works as *2BRO2B*, which takes its title from Hamlet's famous question. Such a question not only plagues Hamlet but Eliot and Vonnegut as well. In Trout's *2BRO2B*, the world has become completely mechanized, all diseases have been cured, and overpopulation threatens humanity's existence. No one seems to have a purpose; few actually have jobs. Because disease no longer exists, death becomes a voluntary event, and to encourage its citizens to choose death, the government creates Ethical Suicide Parlors. A character in the novel proceeds to such a parlor, and before his death he asks if he will see God because he wishes to ask God, "What in hell are people for?" (21). Our Hamlet, the drunken Eliot, longs to know what people are for, and, like Hamlet, he sacrifices his relationship with his love, turns his kingdom on its ear, and attempts to assuage his guilt, in this case for the misdeeds of his ancestors. Eliot goes so far as to write his wife, telling her that "Maybe I flatter myself when I think that I have things in common with Hamlet, that I have an important mission, that I'm temporarily mixed up about how it should be done" (31). Eliot does not stay confused for long, however, and he discovers the nature of his important mission in an unlikely place: a volunteer fire department in Elsinore, California. Before Eliot travels to the heartland and settles in Rosewater, he joins a volunteer fire department—an activity for which Vonnegut also volunteered—and perceives that "they are, when the alarm goes off, almost the only examples of enthusiastic unselfishness to be seen in this land. They rush to the rescue of any human being, and count not the cost. . . . There we have people treasuring people as people. It's extremely rare. So from this we must learn" (184).

In fact, it appears that Eliot learns the most about the ethical treatment of human beings from volunteer firemen and science fiction writers. Eliot is attracted to science fiction writers because they are willing to deal with the philosophical issues that affect every one of us.[11] In proclaiming his love for writers of science fiction, Eliot explains that they are the only writers "with guts enough to really care about the future, who really notice what machines do to us, what wars do to us, what cities do to us, what big, simple ideas do to us, what tremendous misunderstandings, mistakes, accidents and catastrophes do to us" (18). The science fiction writers, who Eliot declares are our hope for the future, write about the very same concerns as Vonnegut; they are less preoccupied with utopian reveries based on technological advances and more concerned with what is best for humanity.

Like volunteer firemen, the science fiction writers Eliot loves best practice their trade in relative anonymity, receiving little income for their work. Indeed, Kilgore Trout is unable to attend the convention in Pennsylvania because he cannot afford to leave his job at a trading stamp redemption center; Trout's fiction sells as filler in pornographic magazines, earning him little or nothing. As is often the case in Vonnegut's world, those who have stories to tell that may improve the life of humanity toil in obscurity and poverty, while those who rule the social and financial worlds spin narratives of injustice and inequity that destroy the human spirit.

Such critics as Allen and Lundquist attack Eliot's vision in *God Bless You, Mr. Rosewater* for its sentimentality and charge him with neglecting the needs of his wife. Allen argues that the novel "reads like a cry from the heart rather than a novel under its author's full intellectual control" (*Understanding* 75), while Lundquist claims that Vonnegut undercuts Eliot's vision by having him wreck "the life of a woman whose only fault had been that she loved him" (44). Allen's assertion that this is a sentimental novel is true enough. But Allen refuses to accept that Vonnegut believes in the heart, that he longs to protect and cherish the human spirit above all else, perhaps sacrificing intellectual control at times. In *God Bless You, Mr. Rosewater*, Vonnegut dreams of a world where his gospel of hope might work, and Eliot, along with Trout, serve as instruments of this most hopeful humanism. Although Eliot's marriage does fail, Lundquist's judgment of Eliot appears to place all of the blame on his shoulders. Lundquist fails, however, to account for Sylvia Rosewater's psychological condition, Samaritrophia. Dr. Ed Brown, the Indianapolis psychiatrist who diagnoses Sylvia's malady, explains that Samaritrophia "is the suppression of an overactive conscience by the rest of the mind" (42). In other words, Sylvia is the product of her father's narratives about culture and class and discrimination; she cannot reconcile herself with Eliot's vision, his mission to help those who need help regardless of ancestry, social status, or hygiene. Eliot longs for a world of mercy and uncritical kindness; Sylvia merely wishes to remain comfortably lodged in her father's narrative of Darwinian justice. Surely Vonnegut does not wish for a world conceived of by Senator Rosewater, a social Darwinist, or Norman Mushari, a lawyer motivated solely by greed. Worlds created by their narratives would likely end in the wasteland Eliot envisions on his way to Indianapolis. Traveling into the city to meet with his wife, Eliot witnesses a firestorm engulfing the Hoosier capital, a firestorm similar to the one that ravaged Dresden, which he had been reading about in *The Bombing of Germany*. Vonnegut's concern with the kinds of narratives that control our culture are rooted in the fiery holocaust that Eliot witnesses. The horrible stories of nationalism and racism, of material progress and virtuous war, that converged to create a situation in which thousands upon thousands were consumed by fire undoubtedly jarred Vonnegut's psyche in a profound and perplexing way. Therefore, Vonnegut's career as a writer may be seen ultimately as a battle against such stories that might allow for the atrocity of some new Dresden. Along with the Eliot Rosewaters of this world, Vonnegut stands firmly for stories of peace and kindness, for stories that heal not maim.

And true to his conviction, Vonnegut ends *God Bless You, Mr. Rosewater* with a movement away from Eliot's horrifying dream of Dresden's destruction, an experience that leaves him in a catatonic state, toward a visionary world of peace and love, one Eliot will propagate with a story that is nothing more than a comforting lie. In the brave new world Eliot envisions, people would be given the power to tell the kinds of stories that build community and selflessness and an enduring love for all life, not simply the lives of the privileged. After spending a year recovering from his harrowing experience when "everything went black . . . , as black as what lay beyond the ultimate rim of the universe" (177), Eliot wakes to the sounds of a bird only to find his position as president of the Rosewater Foundation threatened by the accusation that he is insane. With the help of Kilgore Trout and, surprisingly, Senator Rosewater, Eliot defeats Mushari's efforts to steal the Rosewater fortune by claiming as his own all the children he has supposedly fathered. By once again spreading his arms around the poor, Eliot heals the broken; by embracing Mushari's lie, Eliot serves a higher truth. Not surprisingly, at the hearing to determine whether Eliot is sane, Trout serves as Vonnegut's mouthpiece, declaring Eliot's social activism as an example to all. Using Eliot's lifework, Trout establishes uncritical love as the golden rule of the gospel of hope:

> "It seems to me," said Trout, "that the main lesson Eliot learned is that people can use all the uncritical love they can get."
> "This is *news*?" the Senator raucously inquired.

"It's news that a man was able to *give* that kind of love over a long period of time. If one man can do it, perhaps others can do it, too. It means that our hatred of useless human beings and the cruelties we inflict upon them for their own good need not be parts of human nature. Thanks to the example of Eliot Rosewater millions upon millions of people may learn to love and help whomever they see."

Trout glanced from face to face before speaking his last word on the subject. The last word was: "Joy." (186–87)

Trout and Eliot undermine the grand narratives of American culture, turning its system of ethics upside down. They cannot tolerate a system that ignores human life in its efforts to further Darwinian capitalism or cupidity.

God Bless You, Mr. Rosewater may be the novel most central to Vonnegut's conception of postmodern humanism because it suggests that the purposes often taken up by humanity are mere fabrications. Trout argues that "uselessness will kill strong and weak souls alike" (184); therefore, the most important task before us is to find narratives that create purpose. Such narratives, Trout insists, must move beyond the meaning offered by the stifling, middle-class community of Pisquontuit or the despairing poverty of Rosewater. Our fabrications must ennoble and serve the human spirit, not imprison it. Such is the dream of Trout and Eliot and Vonnegut, a postmodern humanism created out of the patchwork stories of us all. In Cat's Cradle, Vonnegut emphatically argues for the relativity of all stories, the lack of an essential center behind any truth, but in God Bless You, Mr. Rosewater he establishes the one criterion for a postmodern humanism: humanity must be empowered; life must be nurtured. The small narratives we tell, narratives Eliot hopes his progeny will spread as they go into the world and become "fruitful and multiply," must bring light to a world of darkness, a gospel of hope to what Vonnegut often characterizes as a hopeless mess.

Slaughterhouse-Five: The Ethics of Human Atrocity

For twenty-three years Vonnegut attempted to come to grips with the events he witnessed as a soldier in World War II. Like so many writers of his generation, Vonnegut experienced the cataclysmic

affairs of war at the end of his youth, a formative time of philosophical contemplation that was exploded in the incendiary and
violent deaths of 135,000 people living in Dresden. Undoubtedly
the physical and spiritual impact of such a holocaust profoundly
altered Vonnegut's worldview, but, surprisingly, he has on occasion played down the importance of Dresden: "The importance of
Dresden in my life has been considerably exaggerated because my
book about it became a best seller. If the book hadn't been a best
seller, it would seem like a very minor experience in my life"
(Allen, *Conversations* 94). Some critics, Allen among them, have
actually taken Vonnegut's word on the matter, suggesting that
Dresden "was no road-to-Damascus-like conversion" for Vonnegut (Allen, *Understanding* 79). But to accept Vonnegut's assess-
ment of Dresden's importance in his work and personal life
requires the critic to ignore the assertions of contemporary psy-
chology about the severe emotional stress war places on the individual, Vonnegut's own impressive body of work that deals
directly or indirectly with Dresden and the theme of death by
annihilation, and, quite simply, common sense. If we have learned
anything by the end of the twentieth century, it is that war dam-
ages all life; the physical and spiritual destruction of war, the after-
math that festers like an open wound in the years that follow, cannot be shrugged off as inconsequential.[12]

A more honest appraisal of the matter of Dresden occurs later
in the same interview when Vonnegut testifies to the fact that he
has struggled with the memory of Dresden: "There was a complete blank where the bombing of Dresden took place, because I
don't remember. And I looked up several of my war buddies and
they didn't remember, either. They didn't want to talk about it.
There was a complete forgetting of what it was like" (Allen, *Conversations* 94). Vonnegut represses the memory of Dresden and so
much of World War II because of the terror it holds. The very
actions that war demands of the individual are so antithetical to
the normative behavior our culture praises in times of peace that
many people cannot deal with what they have witnessed during
combat action. To remember what has transpired is to relive what
was unbearable in the first place, and, for Vonnegut, this means
dredging the depths of his memory to behold once again the single greatest destruction of human life in modern military history.
It is no wonder that Vonnegut blocked out any recollection of
Dresden. As Paul Fussell explains in *Wartime: Understanding and*

Behavior in the Second World War, "When the war was over, for
most of the participants there was nothing to be said. . . . [M]en of
letters became silent" (134). What does one say about the act of
killing, whether ideologically justified or not? No ideology could
place the events Vonnegut witnessed in a comprehensible pattern;
what remained was merely chaos and silence, and, for over two
decades, Vonnegut worked diligently to make sense out of what is
most nonsensical, most absurd, in human behavior: war.

Therefore, *Slaughterhouse-Five* remains essentially a testament to one man's battle with the demons of war. Much like Hemingway's Nick Adams or Heller's Yossarian, Vonnegut's Billy Pilgrim has been shaken to his very foundation by the bombs of war
and longs to reconcile himself to the experience. But reconciliation
is not to be his. Rather, Billy becomes unstuck in time, traveling to
different moments in his life, as well as to the planet Tralfamadore
where he discovers a coping strategy in the Tralfamadorian conception of time that enables him to work around the war, not
through it. America can offer no grand narrative that makes sense
of the atrocity Billy witnesses in Dresden, and the inhabitants of
Tralfamadore make no attempt to fix meaning to any event, denying any notion of causality. Indeed, the novel itself appears
emphatically and painstakingly to display the failure of traditional
narratives to explain the violation of war. The structure of the
novel—"somewhat in the telegraphic schizophrenic manner of
tales of the planet Tralfamadore"—subverts the notion of causality in its own telling.

For Vonnegut then, Dresden represents his complete disillusionment with the grand narratives of American culture, especially
the narrative of scientific progress in which Vonnegut had innocently placed his trust.[13] After witnessing the awesome power of
science in the service of humanity's hatred, Vonnegut essentially
lost faith:

> But for me it was terrible, after having believed so much in tech-
> nology and having drawn so many pictures of dream automo-
> biles and dream airplanes and dream human dwellings, to see
> the actual use of this technology in destroying a city and killing
> 135,000 people and then to see the even more sophisticated
> technology in the use of nuclear weapons on Japan. I was sick-
> ened by this use of the technology that I had such great hopes
> for. And so I came to fear it. You know, it's like being a devout

Christian and then seeing some horrible massacres conducted by
Christians after a victory. It was a spiritual horror of that sort
which I still carry today. . . . (Allen, *Conversations* 232)

Out of his lost faith, Vonnegut created his most formally postmodern novel to date. The radical shift in form from any modernist conception of the novel results from Vonnegut's struggle to
find a new paradigm for the Dresden experience, one that refused
to be placed in a conventionally modernist narrative.[14] World War
II and the eventual bombing of Dresden, Germany, may be seen as
the results of such absolutism as that about which Bokonon warns
his followers, and for Vonnegut there can be no justification of
such absolutism. Therefore, Vonnegut makes use of metafictional
techniques in order to expose his own struggle with Dresden, and
by doing so he establishes an open relationship with the reader
that allows for more communication than the traditional modernist paradigm. In the first chapter of *Slaughterhouse-Five*, the
author visits his old war buddy Bernard V. O'Hare, in hopes that
their reunion will help him recall the bombing of Dresden. Insert-
ing himself into his created world without comment, Vonnegut
makes no attempt to distinguish between "reality" and "fiction."
During his visit he meets O'Hare's wife Mary, to whom the novel
is dedicated, and Mary, obviously angered by Vonnegut's presence, accuses Vonnegut of attempting to write a book that will
reify the other grand narratives of war:

> "Well, I know," she said. "You'll pretend you were men instead
> of babies, and you'll be played in the movies by Frank Sinatra
> and John Wayne or some of those other glamorous, war-loving,
> dirty old men. And war will look just wonderful, so we'll have
> a lot more of them. And they'll be fought by babies like the
> babies upstairs." (14)

Refusing to accept the metanarratives that her country has offered
in defense and even adulation of the war, Mary O'Hare makes
Vonnegut promise that "there won't be a part for Frank Sinatra or
John Wayne" in his book about Dresden. Not only are there no
parts for the likes of Sinatra and Wayne, the actual bombing of
Dresden never appears in the book.

Instead, Vonnegut tells a petite histoire of the Dresden incident, his own small narrative, or what he calls on the title page,

"A Duty Dance with Death." In order to accommodate what seemingly cannot be accommodated, Vonnegut writes a novel that resembles the books of Tralfamadore, books described as "clumps of symbols" that portray a situation or a scene: "There isn't any particular relationship between all the messages, except that the author has chosen them carefully, so that when seen all at once, they produce an image of life that is beautiful and surprising and deep. There is no beginning, no middle, no end, no suspense, no moral, no causes, no effects" (88). The time shifts in *Slaughter-house-Five* are exactly what prevent the writer and the reader from developing causes and effects, from creating meaning based on a metanarrative; there is a staunch refusal to try to explain how the bombing of Dresden could be justified. Moreover, the refusal to use chronological time represents the deconstruction of one more grand narrative of western civilization; the idea behind chronological time as an organizing principle is to show the linear progression, the causes and the effects, of "history." Because Billy Pilgrim believes that this commitment to time as linear is the cause of humanity's woeful condition, he sets out, as any good optometrist would, to give Earthlings corrected vision. He writes in a letter to the newspaper:

> The most important thing I learned on Tralfamadore was that when a person dies he only appears to die. He is still very much alive in the past. . . . It is just an illusion we have here on Earth that one moment follows another one, like beads on a string, and that once a moment is gone it is gone forever. (26–27)

Billy Pilgrim's refusal to see time as moments following one another like "beads on a string" suggests an interesting alternative to the postmodern condition, an alternative that turns away from a Western conception of time to tell its own petite histoire, one affording us the chance to see "an image of life that is beautiful and surprising and deep" (88).

But does Billy's conception of time truly offer little more than the allusive façade of dreams, of science fiction? The answer to this question may be found in Vonnegut's own response to the war and in an examination of Billy's sanity. We must not forget that Vonnegut plays a crucial role in the first and last chapters of the novel and that Billy's response to Dresden does not represent Vonnegut's own response. While it is true that both Vonnegut and Billy tell their stories in order to cope with the darkness that threatens to engulf them, it remains a common mistake to conflate the two. Thomas Wymer argues convincingly that the lessons Billy learns from the Tralfamadorians about the nature of suffering and death in the universe do not embody Vonnegut's own convictions. Indeed, Vonnegut warns against the very kind of fatalism that the Tralfamadorians preach, consistently pointing out that the creatures who embrace such a philosophy are machines. Machines do not reflect the inner workings of humanity, and Vonnegut, of all people, would never suggest that humanity take its cues from any of science's great achievements, especially machines. In the fifth chapter Vonnegut makes it clear why Billy and Eliot Rosewater turn to the writing of Kilgore Trout to solve their crises: "They had both found life meaningless, partly because of what they had seen in war. . . . So they were trying to re-invent themselves and their universe. Science fiction was a big help" (101). And science fiction is, indeed, what Billy uses to cope with what Broer characterizes as his schizophrenic condition. Science fiction, quite simply, offers Billy a chance to escape the confines of his grim and macabre existence. To come unstuck in time is to be free of any earthly shackle, and the conventions of slick science fiction can present no more cliché or unrealistic a fantasy life than the planet Tralfamadore, replete with a sultry, Hollywood starlet in the form of Montana Wildhack. Time travel is Billy's therapy; his stories are his delusions.

Conversely, Vonnegut uses writing as a form of therapy and social protest. Unlike Billy, Vonnegut never loses sight of the physical reality of war in the telling of his tale. Very early on Vonnegut admits that antiwar books are as effective as antiglacier books. The reality remains that there will always be war. And in the carnage of war, we will find the names of the victims and their stories, and out of humanity's violent refuse will come the survivors marked by the scars of living and their longing to forget what will forever haunt them. But Vonnegut, the optimist and the survivor, will not be daunted. He must write about Dresden; the ethics of human atrocity compel him to speak out against the insanity of war, to affirm the value of all life. In the first chapter, which echoes Benjamin Franklin's address to his son in *The Autobiography*, Vonnegut instructs his own sons against the practices of massacres:

> I have told my sons that they are not under any circum-
> stances to take part in massacres, and that the news of massacres
> of enemies is not to fill them with satisfaction or glee.
>
> I have also told them not to work for companies which
> make massacre machinery, and to express contempt for people
> who think we need machinery like that. (19)

Such words are not the words of a fatalist. After writing thousands and thousands of pages over two decades about World War
II, Vonnegut refuses to make sense of Dresden and refuses to
acquiesce to any notion of war; he throws away all he has written
because as a "trafficker in climaxes and thrills and characterization and wonderful dialogue and suspense and confrontations"
(*Slaughterhouse-Five* 5), he cannot fit the reality of his experience
into a conventional work of fiction. As Vonnegut says to his editor, Sam Lawrence, "there is nothing intelligent to say about a
massacre. Everybody is supposed to be dead, to never say anything or want anything" (19). And so the story spins its wheels
before us: bewildering in its form, dazzling in its aspirations. We
witness Vonnegut making attempt after attempt to outline the
story of Dresden, creating the most beautiful storyline on the back
of some wallpaper with his daughter's crayons, but much to Vonnegut's surprise, a book about Dresden will require far more of
him than simply "report[ing] what I had seen" (2), and, of course,
the crayon-colored outline inevitably fails.

Vonnegut's inability to speak cogently and coherently about
Dresden represents the ethics of human atrocity. In *From the Kingdom of Memory*, Elie Wiesel suggests that the survivor speaks
words, writes words, reluctantly, that writing for the survivor is
not a profession, but a calling. In a moving passage, Wiesel
explains, "I never intended to be a novelist. The only role I sought
was that of witness. I believed that, having survived by chance, I
was duty-bound to give meaning to my survival, to justify each
moment of my life. I knew the story had to be told. Not to trans-
mit an experience is to betray it" (14). The ethics of human atrocity are created out of the need to testify to such experiences as the
Holocaust and the fire-bombing of Dresden. As Wiesel claims, not
to tell the story of survival is to betray it, and such a betrayal is as
much a betrayal of self as it is a betrayal of those who perished.
Therefore, if Vonnegut had proceeded to tell a conventional story
about his time in Dresden, a story that reified the ideology of war,

he would have committed an act of treason against all those long dead, their bones delivered into the earth, as well as an act of treason against all those who survive, their souls shattered. For this reason, Vonnegut's narrative is a failure by his own admission, a failure by modernist standards for the novel: "This one is a failure, and had to be, since it was written by a pillar of salt" (*Slaughterhouse-Five* 22). To look back, to testify against the crimes of humanity, remains the only ethical choice for Vonnegut. In his testimony, he becomes nothing more than the salt of the earth, a pillar like Lot's wife. Vonnegut's choice to look beyond the pale, back toward the fruits of humanity's evil, gives to us a book of remarkable beauty. *Slaughterhouse-Five*, born out of one man's honest and human response to the carnage of our brutality, out of his rage against the sickness of war, endures as a paragon of postmodern morality.

3

Apocalyptic Grumbling

Postmodern Righteousness in the Late Novels

As I approached my fiftieth birthday, I had become more and more enraged and mystified by the idiot decisions made by my countrymen. And then I had come suddenly to pity them, for I understood how innocent and natural it was for them to behave so abominably, with such abominable results: They were doing their best to live like people invented in story books. This was the reason Americans shot each other so often: It was a convenient literary device for ending short stories and books.

Why were so many Americans treated by their government as though their lives were as disposable as paper facial tissues? Because that was the way authors customarily treated bit-part players in their made-up tales.

Once I understood what was making America such a dangerous, unhappy nation of people who had nothing to do with real life, I resolved to shun storytelling. I would write about life.

—Kurt Vonnegut, *Conversations with Kurt Vonnegut*

Breakfast of Champions: Exorcising the Demons

THE COMPLETION OF *Slaughterhouse-Five* marks a definite and profound turning point in Vonnegut's fictional world. After working toward the cataclysmic events of Dresden for much of his career and finally walking through its flames with the writing of *Slaughterhouse-Five*, Vonnegut stood before the yawning chasm of the blank page with no clear direction. Motionless and bound by his tragic vision of humanity, Vonnegut was at a loss. There was seemingly nothing more to say, and for the next four years he published no new fiction. Having walked many miles to reach the literary fame *Slaughterhouse-Five* bestowed upon him, Vonnegut faced a spiritual crossroads. As he explains,

> Well, I felt after I finished *Slaughterhouse-Five* that I didn't have to write at all anymore if I didn't want to. It was the end of some sort of career. I don't know why, exactly. I suppose that flowers when they're through blooming, have some sort of awareness of some purpose having been served. Flowers didn't ask to be flowers and I didn't ask to be me. At the end of *Slaughterhouse-Five*, I had the feeling that I had produced this blossom. So I had a shutting-off feeling, you know, that I had done what I was supposed to do and everything was OK. And that was the end of it. I could figure out my missions for myself after that. (Allen, *Conversations* 107)

In 1970, Vonnegut took an unexpected turn onto a road he had up to this time never traveled professionally: his new mission was to be theatre. Vonnegut's first play, *Happy Birthday, Wanda June*, which featured such noted actors as Marsha Mason and Kevin McCarthy, opened to mixed reviews.[1] Admittedly, Vonnegut's turn to drama had more to do with the middle-life changes he faced than with some grand artistic vision that only the stage would accommodate. Vonnegut's marriage was slowly drawing to a close, his children were grown and out of the house, and, as he puts it in the preface to the published version of the play, "I was drinking more and arguing a lot, and I had to get out of that house" (vii). But apparently the dramatic arts did not appease his inner struggle, and, in *Breakfast of Champions*, we find Vonnegut journeying ever more deeply into his fictional world to be born again.

The forces involved in Vonnegut's spiritual crisis came from within and without, and his first response—the move from Cape Cod to New York City—led only to his further isolation and an increasingly tempestuous struggle with the meaning and value of human existence. As Vonnegut reveals in *Palm Sunday*, his move to New York City was his attempt to start all over again, but what actually transpired "is a tale of a man's cold sober flight into unpopulated nothingness. The booze and women, good and bad, are likely to come along in time, but nothingness is the first seductress—again, the little death" (304–05). And at the center of the book he wrote during this dark time lies both physical and spiritual death. As Vonnegut remarks, "Suicide is at the heart of the book" (Allen, *Conversations* 108). But suicide, in the end, does not envelop the author or his characters with its deceitful veil; rather, by entering his own work and following to its dark conclusion the mechanistic and fatalistic philosophy found in Kilgore Trout's *Now It Can Be Told*, Vonnegut faces his greatest fears only to rediscover his commitment to the life of the human spirit in the paintings of Rabo Karabekian.[2]

Although Vonnegut's first six novels develop a moral commitment to humanity, that commitment, driven by faith, remains tenuous throughout his career. At no time does Vonnegut become comfortable with the notion that humanity represents the highest achievement of some mythical creator, that our actions are uniquely predestined in some providential plan. Instead, he strives to make sense of our existence, to understand better how he should live in a world absurdly committed to its own destruction. Against the canvas of such destruction, Vonnegut writes novels, as he explains, "to make myself like life better than I do. . . . People will believe anything, which means I will believe anything. I learned that in anthropology. I want to start believing in things that have shapeliness and harmony" (Allen, *Conversations* 109).
· Before he can focus on those things that have shapeliness and harmony, however, he must do battle with those forces that destroy the human spirit and in turn destroy the earth. Therefore, in the preface to *Breakfast of Champions*, Vonnegut explains that he must make his head as empty as it was when he "was born onto this damaged planet fifty years ago" (5). And Vonnegut advocates such a plan for us all: "I suspect that this is something most white Americans, and nonwhite Americans who imitate white Americans, should do. The things other people have put into my head,

at any rate, do not fit together nicely, are often useless and ugly, are out of proportion with one another . . . I have no culture, no humane harmony in my brains" (5). The key to Vonnegut's attack, his postmodern crusade against all kinds of spiritual and physical abuses, rests in his devotion to a "humane harmony." The only way we will learn to care humanely for the earth and one another is by coming to grips with what it means to be human.

The dramatic tension on which Vonnegut builds *Breakfast of Champions* consists of its author's struggle to embrace once again a narrative that attempts to describe the value of the human spirit. As in *Slaughterhouse-Five*, Vonnegut inserts himself as a character into his own artistic creation. In *Breakfast of Champions*, however, Vonnegut the author pushes the limits of metafictional art. Rather than appearing simply in the introductory and concluding chapters in order to explain to the reader what the book attempts to do, in *Breakfast of Champions* Vonnegut makes his own fictional epiphany central to the story. While this might not prove problematic in examining the work of some artists, because of Vonnegut's assertion that life itself is a fiction, that all we have are comforting lies, it becomes difficult to discern where the flesh-and-blood author ends and his fictional doppelgänger begins. Moreover, by using such a fictional technique, Vonnegut seems to be mocking our efforts to delineate the boundaries between the world of fiction and the world of fact; in the narrative scheme of *Breakfast of Champions*, he once again asserts that we are what we pretend to be. Consequently, if Vonnegut pretends to be an author in his own novel, then indeed he is that author. Therefore, when Vonnegut speaks as the fictional narrator of the novel, he in fact speaks for himself. For this reason, it is not unusual to find Vonnegut giving the same speeches in interviews that he gives as a character in his own novels. Unlike other artists, Vonnegut does indeed conflate the two realities, an indulgence that seems logical to this postmodern harlequin. Not surprisingly, then, Vonnegut finds his narrative of hope in the very work of art he has created himself, and, in this novel, all roads lead to the Midland City Arts Festival.

Along the way to Midland City, however, Vonnegut takes on the history and practices of American culture in an attempt to destroy those narratives that dehumanize and damage life on this planet. Because Vonnegut focuses his narrative on the shameful practices of our culture, the plot of *Breakfast of Champions* is loosely constructed; the climactic meeting of Dwayne Hoover and Kilgore Trout remains a simple plot device that enables him to satirize our devotion to nonsensical and, at times, terribly harmful narratives. After outlining the history of America in a voice that is childlike in its directness and honesty, Vonnegut dismantles the notion that any of this has led to democracy:

> The undippable flag was a beauty, and the anthem and the vacant motto might not have mattered much, if it weren't for this: a lot of citizens were so ignored and cheated and insulted that they thought they might be in the wrong country, or even on the wrong planet, that some terrible mistake had been made. It might have comforted them some if their anthem and their motto had mentioned fairness or brotherhood or hope or happiness, had somehow welcomed them to the society and its real estate. (9)

According to Vonnegut, much of this is simply playful and innocent "nonsense," but what concerns him is the spread of harmful nonsense in the form of lies told to children by their teachers. The fact that children are told that our continent was discovered in 1492 distresses Vonnegut. He explains that "The teachers told the children that this was when their continent was discovered by human beings. Actually, millions of human beings were already living full and imaginative lives on the continent in 1492. That was simply the year in which sea pirates began to cheat and rob and kill them" (10). Ultimately, what Vonnegut finds most disturbing about the history taught to children in America is the idea that "the sea pirates eventually created a government which became a beacon of freedom to human beings everywhere else" (10). Vonnegut claims that what was actually created was a nation where the sea pirates owned human slaves: "They used human beings for machinery, and, even after slavery was eliminated, because it was so embarrassing, they and their descendants continued to think of ordinary human beings as machines" (11). And, once again, Vonnegut the postmodern preacher of humanism decries the mechanization of humanity. In fact, *Breakfast of Champions* may be seen as a righteous lament over our abuse of the land and its people, over the sacrifices we have made to build an economic machine that, in the end, can only consume the earth and all it sustains. Facing such a grim reality, Vonnegut, like Dwayne, searches for some reason to see people as anything but machines that perpetuate the folly of this destructive American narrative.

In an attempt to understand why humans have become mere cogs in the automaton called America, Vonnegut experiments with the traditional form and rhetoric of the genre of the novel. His use of an arrestingly simple and didactic prose style and the culmination of narrative movement in Midland City where he witnesses the violent outcome of Dwayne's schizophrenic condition represent Vonnegut's efforts to understand how he has come to this point in his life and how he might empty his head of American culture's plastic façade. Quintessentially postmodern in form, *Breakfast of Champions* recognizes no fictional boundaries; from the preface to the final drawing of the author shedding a tear, Vonnegut hammers away at our notion of truth in fiction and fiction in truth. The penultimate metafictional moment occurs when Vonnegut has an extended conversation with Trout and then proceeds to set his creation free. In addition, Vonnegut, who latter in life actually put on a one-man show of his illustrations at an art gallery in New York, uses his drawings to connect the reader in the most elemental way to the artifacts of American culture. Jerome Klinkowitz suggests that as we view the drawings, "We are at once reminded of the simple essence of a thing, and also of its inexorability. *There it is*, says the text, in a manner so plain that we are forced to see what rhetoric and myth obscures" (*Kurt Vonnegut* 71). Perhaps one of the most provocative and offensive drawings in the book depicts a woman's open vagina. The drawing, however, illustrates perfectly the kind of work Vonnegut hopes to accomplish; paradoxically, by using that which dehumanizes, Vonnegut hopes to draw the reader back into the circle of humanity. Not surprisingly, this picture, among other drawings and passages, has been the target of censorship by many religious and ideologically conservative parties.[3] But what these people fail to grasp is that Vonnegut himself, by illustrating in an extremely crude and simple manner, subverts practices such as pornography that dehumanize. When Vonnegut explains that a "wide-open beaver was a photograph of a woman not wearing underpants, and with her legs far apart, so that the mouth of her vagina could be seen" (22), he deliberately uses flat, objective language; like a social scientist, he chronicles the ridiculous and lurid devotion of so many Americans to pornography.[4] The drawing of the "large rodent" that "loved water, so it built dams" (23), that is juxta-

posed with the drawing of the vaginal orifice serves as the moralistic punch line for Vonnegut's social critique. By holding a mirror
up to the face of America, in this case to its odd obsession with the
photographing of female genitalia, Vonnegut suggests that with
the use of machines like cameras we have removed what makes us
human. He corrects this perception by telling us that what we are
really looking at when we view pornography of this kind is the
place from which all human life must come, or, as the caption
beneath his drawing explains, "This was where babies came
from" (23). Pornography obliterates the beauty of the human
spirit that Vonnegut will eventually rediscover in the paintings of
Karabekian. The pornographic pictures that are the companion
pieces to so much of Trout's fiction function as a tool of despair
in a culture that encourages the machinelike exploitation of flesh.

Finally, *Breakfast of Champions* refutes any notion that
humans are expendable. Dwayne's illness, the result of bad chem-
icals, is nonetheless lethal to all concerned. In no uncertain terms,
Vonnegut dismisses the mechanistic and fatalistic reverie that drives Dwayne to see all humans, except himself, as robots. In his
righteous crusade against American culture, Vonnegut seems to be
saying that our problems—environmental, social, personal—stem
from narratives that view people as machinery. And, of course,
Vonnegut has been haunted by such thoughts his entire career. As
a writer, Vonnegut's mind has been possessed by the demonic
voices of an American culture bent on its own destruction, and,
with great effort and the help of Karabekian, he hopes to exorcise
his past in order to help create a more hopeful future. It is
Karabekian, Vonnegut's own creation, who enables Vonnegut to
believe once again in humanity and the important role art plays in
nurturing the life of the mind and spirit. Late in the novel, while
attending the Midland City Arts Festival, Vonnegut confesses in a
moment of crisis that he has no respect for the creative works of
Karabekian or Beatrice Keedsler:

> I thought Karabekian with his meaningless pictures had entered
> into a conspiracy with millionaires to make poor people feel stu-
> pid. I thought Beatrice Keedsler had joined hands with other
> old-fashioned storytellers to make people believe that life had
> leading characters, minor characters, significant details, insignif-
> icant details, that it had lessons to be learned, tests to be passed,
> and a beginning, a middle, and an end. (209)

What Vonnegut longs for is a world where every person is "exactly as important as any other" (210); such a world, he hopes, will destroy the abuses of war, of slavery, of environmental rape. Vonnegut so adamantly opposes "old-fashioned storytellers" because their form of storytelling establishes narratives and a narrative form that help create the nightmarish condition of the present. Concerning the art of Karabekian, however, Vonnegut is mistaken. Although Vonnegut expects to learn nothing from Karabekian, whom he considers "a vain and weak and trashy man, no artist at all" (220), it is Karabekian who transforms him into "the serene Earthling which I am this day" (220). What Vonnegut discovers—in the spiritual climax of the book identified by Vonnegut as such in a humorous metafictional moment—is that Karabekian's paintings do exactly what he hopes his own writing may do: depict life without leaving anything important out. In a lengthy speech delivered to the cocktail lounge guests, Karabekian describes his painting, *The Temptation of St. Anthony*. It consists of a vertical stripe of orange reflecting tape on a field of green wall paint, and he vows

> that the picture your city owns shows everything about life which truly matters, with nothing left out. It is a picture of the awareness of every animal. It is the immaterial core of every animal— the "I am" to which all messages are sent. It is all that is alive in any of us—in a mouse, in a deer, in a cocktail waitress. It is unwavering and pure, no matter what preposterous adventure may befall us. A sacred picture of Saint Anthony alone is one vertical, unwavering band of light. If a cockroach were near him, or a cocktail waitress, the picture would show two such bands of light. Our awareness is all that is alive and maybe sacred in any of us. Everything else about us is dead machinery. (221)

And out of this epiphany, Vonnegut is healed. By embracing the light, the sacred awareness in all living things, not merely human, Vonnegut finds the courage to go on writing. Karabekian's painting offers one more narrative that Vonnegut may use to preach his postmodern humanism. Vonnegut knows that there is no certainty, no factual data, asserting the existence of life's unwavering band of light, but by reaching out to touch it in faith, he celebrates its possibility and, as the book's epigraph suggests, "comes forth as gold."

Slapstick: Laboring for Love,
or at Least Some Common Decency

Where *Breakfast of Champions* ends, *Slapstick* begins. After struggling through much of *Breakfast of Champions* to find some confirmation that life on Earth is worth preserving, Vonnegut breaks free of doubt and in *Slapstick* immediately goes to work on improving the human condition. The condition of humanity, however, appears to be moving ever closer to its own ruination. Armed with a new narrative of hope, Vonnegut leaves Midland City to write novels that take on this world's miserable state of affairs. But the world seems relatively uninterested in Vonnegut's transformation. In a review of *Slapstick*, Loree Rackstraw characterizes Vonnegut's work as a "crusade for human dignity and decency" (189), while Klinkowitz, in another review of the book, suggests that Vonnegut, in the face of life's madness, "chooses to be: unalienated, self-effacing, funny, and comforting" (188). But judging by the critical voices of other book reviewers and academics, there is no clear consensus about the importance of Vonnegut's later work. In fact, it appears that many of them wish for none of the comforts Vonnegut describes, or, as he puts it, most people are "sick enough to want an end to life" (Allen, *Conversations* 236).

By 1976, the honeymoon between Vonnegut and his critical audience was over. The attack that followed the release of *Slapstick* appeared to be nothing short of a witch hunt. The magic Vonnegut had once worked in books like *Cat's Cradle* and *Slaughterhouse-Five* was now deemed by some critics as nothing more than a charlatan's tricks. As Vonnegut explains in an interview:

> *Slapstick* may be a very bad book. I am perfectly willing to believe that. Everybody else writes lousy books, so why shouldn't I? What was unusual about the reviews was that they wanted people to admit now that I had never been any good. The reviewer for the Sunday *Times* actually asked critics who had praised me in the past to now admit in public how wrong they'd been. My publisher, Sam Lawrence, tried to comfort me by saying that authors were invariably attacked when they became fabulously well-to-do. (184)

Lawrence, in his desire to comfort his most celebrated and financially successful author, cuts to the heart of the matter. Such censure as Vonnegut received after the unprecedented critical and financial success of *Slaughterhouse-Five* may be explained by a single rule: critics dislike or turn on the work of those artists who become beloved by a popular audience. Not surprisingly, what so many critics find wanting in *Slapstick* are the very characteristics praised as revolutionary in the earlier fiction. For example, Vonnegut's use of three different points of view in the novel is now regarded at best as distracting and at worst uncontrolled. The shifting points of view, however, function in much the same way as they did in *Breakfast of Champions*. Likewise, many critics attack another formal feature, the repetition of a single phrase, here "Hi ho." Allen claims that a "telling example of the exhaustion of Vonnegut's imagination in *Slapstick* is his tired refrain of 'Hi ho'" (*Understanding* 119). But what Allen and other critics fail to acknowledge is that Vonnegut continually plays with the conventions of fiction, including his own. In the use of "Hi ho," Vonnegut parodies his own use of repetitive phrases in the two previous novels. In *Slapstick*, Wilbur actually displays his own annoyance with the convention. In a metafictional moment that suggests Vonnegut may have grown weary of "So it goes," used in *Slaughterhouse-Five*, Wilbur says, "I swear: If I live to complete this autobiography, I will go through it again, and cross out all the 'Hi ho's.' Hi ho" (32). But Vonnegut did have appreciative reviewers. Perhaps the most telling and balanced estimation of *Slapstick* comes from the pen of one of America's most respected authors, John Updike. The title of his review, "All's Well in Skyscraper National Park," suggests that, indeed, nothing has gone awry in Vonnegut's art. Moreover, Updike claims that the project of dealing with the pain served up by modern life that Vonnegut began in his short stories published in *Collier's* and the *Saturday Evening Post* continues in his latest effort, appropriately set in Manhattan, where the best and worst civilization has to offer collides all too often in absurd and comic ways. What many critics have railed against in Vonnegut's fiction as infantile prose on sophomoric subjects, Updike argues, is an important and deliberate creation that "looks easy only in retrospect" (47).

The creation that lies at the eye of the fictional maelstrom called *Slapstick* is the extended family. Actually, the entire novel laments the loss of family and community in America. At fifty-two years of age, Vonnegut found his family had been reduced in number by his divorce and the deaths of most of his maternal and paternal relatives. Thus, as he began writing his eighth novel, he found himself in the midst of one of the most populated cities in the world fighting loneliness. In the book's prologue, as has been his habit since the revelatory preface to *Mother Night*, Vonnegut speaks directly to the reader about the motivation behind the novel and its eventual production. The transparency of such moments represents Vonnegut's continued efforts to move beyond the boundaries established by traditional fiction. As a postmodernist he is at all times conscious of the artificial nature of his enterprise, but, as a moralist who wishes to serve as a useful cell in the body politic, he labors to include the reader in the composition of the fictional moment. In a sense, Vonnegut's use of metafiction establishes a reading family of sorts by bringing us all into the game of storytelling; the social benefits that result undoubtedly please Vonnegut. But there is more. In the prologue, Vonnegut reveals to the reader that *Slapstick* "is the closest I will ever come to writing an autobiography" (1). Triggering a fantastical memoir is the death of Vonnegut's Uncle Alex. Flying with his brother Bernard to Indianapolis where the funeral was to be held, Vonnegut realizes that this Midwestern city that once housed the Vonnegut clan no longer seems like home. Instead, Indianapolis stands vacant, a town like any other town in middle America. What had once seemed inevitable for all Vonneguts—the eventual return to Indianapolis to take one's place in the family business and to care for one another with familial affection and decency—now is merely a distant memory.

As is only fitting for an autobiography, such memories, especially of Vonnegut's sister Alice, inundate *Slapstick*. On the plane, looking at the vacant seat between Bernard and himself, Vonnegut says, "It could have been a seat for our sister Alice, whose age was halfway between mine and Bernard's. She wasn't in that seat and on her way to her beloved Uncle Alex's funeral, for she had died among strangers in New Jersey, of cancer—at the age of forty-one" (11). Vonnegut tells us that she is the person for whom he has written all these years, and claims it is because of her, his ideal reader, that his artistic vision possesses any unity at all. Because of his love for his sister, a condition he would rather call "common decency," Vonnegut is driven to look for some means to fill the void left by her death and his shrinking family of relatives in Indianapolis. For Vonnegut, these feelings work as effectively as rationality in directing his themes. In *Love's Knowledge*, Martha Nussbaum claims that there is ethical value to emotions, especially love, and the view of rationality that suggests emotions in some way mar productive thought is erroneous. She concludes that emotions are frequently more reliable and less deceptively seductive than intellectual calculations. Moreover, Nussbaum suggests that because "the emotions have this cognitive dimension in their very structure, it is very natural to view them as intelligent parts of our ethical agency, responsive to the workings of deliberation and essential to its completion" (40–41). As if from the ethical structure Nussbaum describes, Vonnegut produces this work, as he has much of his other work, out of an emotional response to what he sees as life's inane workings. What is important to Vonnegut when dealing with our all-too-often cruel and humorless world, he says, is "Bargaining in good faith with destiny" (*Slapstick* 2). His sister's destiny, her cruel and protracted bout with cancer, roils within him. But, as he recounts in the novel's first pages, Alice did, indeed, bargain in good faith with her destiny, and, toward the end of her life, when death was imminent, she described her demise in painfully humorous terms as "Soap Opera!" and "Slapstick" (11). For Vonnegut, the pain caused by her death settles just under the surface of the novel. Updike claims that in *Slapstick*, "Vonnegut's abashed and constant sorrow breaks through to touch the reader" (43), but it does so more because of the immediate family he has known and lost than because of the extended family he dreams we all might have. What *Slapstick* offers then is a means for combating loneliness. Vonnegut knows that he is not the only one to feel loss, and out of his compassion, his desire to treat others with common decency, he dreams of extended families where no one would suffer the loneliness that our society ignores as it feeds an economic machine that by its very nature fragments families.

While at first it may seem odd to compare Vonnegut's ideas concerning family and community with those of the farmer and man of letters Wendell Berry, it becomes increasingly clear that their moral and social agendas are surprisingly similar. In 1964, Berry made the decision to leave New York University, where he held a teaching position, in order to return to his ancestral home in Kentucky. There since that time he has reclaimed the family farm and written over twenty-seven books of fiction, poetry, and prose. He suggests in several of his essays that the most destructive element in our culture is the machinery of an economy that insists on transience. Like Vonnegut, Berry protests the increasing mechanization of our culture and its subsequent disregard for the physical and spiritual well-being of the land and those it sustains. As Berry explains, few people have recognized "the connection between the 'modernization' of agricultural techniques and the disintegration of the culture and the communities of farming— and the consequent disintegration of the structures of urban life. What we have called agricultural progress has, in fact, involved the forcible displacement of millions of people" (*Unsettling* 41). Such displacement is the nature of our times. At the beginning of the twenty-first century, we are a nation of moving vans and sub-divisions built quickly of prefabricated parts and by construction workers from half a world away. Transience seems to be our inheritance. In order to find professional success that offers some small semblance of financial security, we are forced to leave behind our familial and cultural roots, to move at a moment's notice as we are awarded the next promotion. As Vonnegut explains in an interview:

> Well I'm used to the rootlessness that goes with my profession. But I would like people to be able to stay in one community for a lifetime, to travel away from it to see the world, but always to come home again. . . . Until recent times, you know, human beings usually had a permanent community of relatives. They had dozens of homes to go to. So when a married couple had a fight, one or the other could go to a house three doors down and stay with a close relative until he was feeling tender again. Or if a kid got so fed up with his parents that he couldn't stand it, he could march over to his uncle's for a while. And this is no longer possible. Each family is locked into its little box. The neighbors aren't relatives. There aren't other houses where people can go and be cared for. (Allen, *Conversations* 79–80)

While Berry attempts to reform this problem by crusading for a return to diversified agricultural practices, Vonnegut looks to an anthropologically designed social plan. Because of the extent to which America has become dependent upon the economic structures of factory production and its place politically and economically in the world market, Vonnegut sees no possibilities for a return to the life experienced by most Americans at the turn of the nineteenth century. Instead, he proposes a plan that might be implemented as easily as the distribution of Social Security numbers. It is a plan based on the structure of Dr. Robert Redfield's folk society, but designed to accommodate the patterns of life we find at the beginning of this century.[5]

Vonnegut's plan, outlined in the novel's fictional account of Wilbur Swain's life, involves the creation of extended families by the government. Before Wilbur is forcibly removed from his twin sister, Eliza, the two grotesquely deformed but brilliant children envision a world without loneliness. By literally putting their heads together—an act in which their minds form a single genius—they come up with, the novel claims, some of the most important scientific and social advances the world has ever known. Eventually, the Chinese, under the direction of Eliza, come to retrieve the writings of the two Swain children, but Eliza and Wilbur's plan to create extended families remains safely intact with Wilbur. After graduating from Harvard, Wilbur runs for and is elected the president of the United States. His campaign slogan, "Lonesome No More," refers to his promise to give everyone in the United States an extended family. Extended families are created randomly by replacing the middle name of every citizen with a series of names like Daffodil or Raspberry; those people with corresponding middle names immediately become a relative of some sort. What Wilbur and Vonnegut hope to solve with the proliferation of relatives is our lack of community. With extended families in place, whenever people move or find themselves in a strange place on their travels or need some kind of help, the family is there. Of course, Vonnegut does acknowledge that some family members are more generous than others, but he concludes that with enough family members there is always some relative who fits the bill.[6]

But Wilbur's plan fails. In the course of the novel, the world as we know it goes, quite simply, to hell. America no longer exists as a democratic nation, and in its place kingdoms proliferate; because of tampering by scientists, the gravity on Earth fluctuates, destroying all manmade structures and making flight impossible; the Green Death and the Albanian Flu decimate the population, and Manhattan, where Swain resides, becomes an isolated island of ruins. None of these catastrophes, however, results from the leadership of Swain; rather, they are the residual products of those grand narratives against which Vonnegut has fought since his career began. Indeed, the only light in this postapocalyptic landscape radiates from the relationships provided by the extended families that Wilbur helps establish just before the fall of the American government. In the end, only love, or common decency, remains.

To the surprise of many critics, love and common decency are, indeed, the myths on which Vonnegut constructs the narrative of *Slapstick*. In *Vonnegut in America*, Reed remarks, "Through all of the slapstick mocking of the idea . . . some reasonably serious defense of extended families survives" (177). In fact, as hard as some may find it to believe, Vonnegut remains, if nothing else, a fictional activist of sorts. Although some may consider such work a weakness in the realm of art, Vonnegut nonetheless soberly addresses our current state of human affairs and works diligently to offer comforting narratives. Without becoming dogmatic or preachy—slapstick humor seldom allows for any piety—Vonnegut continually pushes us to consider ways in which we may improve the world. Out of his own personal loss, Vonnegut bargains in good faith, and like Laurel and Hardy, to whom the novel is dedicated, his grotesque, situational comedy not only leads to laughter but to the realization that a life led without the love and compassion, the common decency, that only true community offers is surely no life at all.

Jailbird: Vonnegut's Sermon on the Mount

After the damaging reviews of *Breakfast of Champions* and *Slapstick*, Vonnegut began a new phase in his career by practicing what can only be called postmodern social realism. His last five novels, with the exception of *Galápagos*, all weave their texts with the texts of American history, but never lose sight of the constructed nature of reality. By using first-person narration, often delivered by guilt-ridden men who have stood at the fringes of important political and cultural events, Vonnegut has revealed our flawed progress as a nation while condemning the narratives of nationalism and greed that have made a mockery of our Constitutional ideals. Because of the sweeping flood of ill will from critics, however, many have neglected the novels that follow *Slapstick*, and the lack of attention proves unfortunate in light of the social vision reflected in the art that Vonnegut has produced in this second phase of his career.

In *Jailbird*, American history drives the actions of all the players. In fact, the novel includes a four-page index of all the historical and fictional persons found within this modern-day morality play. At the same time, however, Vonnegut underscores the constructed nature of history—denying any notion of an essential reality behind the discourse—by attributing human agency to specific years: "Pay attention, please, for years as well as people are characters in this book, which is the story of my life so far. Nineteen-hundred and Thirteen gave me the gift of life. Nineteen-hundred and Twenty-nine wrecked the American economy. Nineteen-hundred and Thirty-one sent me to Harvard" (1). Perhaps what triggers Vonnegut's new turn toward historically accurate and socially active postmodern realism is his recognition that those stories that might truly affect our world for the better too often flounder between the leaves of history books lost to so many generations. The history at the center of *Jailbird* involves the tragic demise of Sacco and Vanzetti, two common laborers put to death in the electric chair after having been falsely convicted of murder. Their deaths strike Vonnegut as especially poignant and unjust because of the confession of Celestino Madeiros, who claimed to have committed the murder for which Sacco and Vanzetti were sentenced to death. Ironically, along with the other two immigrants, Madeiros was electrocuted. Vonnegut spends much of the prologue to *Jailbird* recounting this history, and, toward the end of the novel, he has Walter Starbuck bemoan the loss of such a moving passage in the life of our nation. Too many people, according to Walter, know nothing of Sacco and Vanzetti. The loss of such stories as this is especially tragic, Walter's memorable narrative suggests, because it is in their retelling that we find our hope to improve the condition of humanity. As Kathryn Hume argues, Walter sets out to show "what an individual can do to alleviate the pain inherent in the human condition" (442), but without narratives of hope born of the sacrifice of those who fight against oppression there can be no movement forward. Silence not only destroys the past but also the future, and, at sixty-six, Walter still believes "that peace and plenty and happiness can be worked out some way" (14). Therefore, with faith and a vision of some brighter future, Walter proceeds to tell the story of Sacco and Vanzetti to Israel Edel, a PhD in history who has never heard of the two laborers and confuses them with Leopold and Loeb:

> When I was a young man, I expected the story of Sacco and Vanzetti to be retold as often and as movingly, to be as irresistible, as the story of Jesus Christ some day. Weren't modern

people, if they were to marvel creatively at their own lifetimes, I thought, entitled to a Passion like Sacco and Vanzetti's, which ended in an electric chair?

As for the last days of Sacco and Vanzetti as a modern Passion: As on Golgotha, three lower-class men were executed at the same time by a state. This time, though, not just one of the three was innocent. This time two of the three were innocent. (171–72)

Their innocence inspires Vonnegut to search for some narrative that can lead to a world redeemed by such sacrifice. The alleged crime of Sacco and Vanzetti, as Vonnegut sees it, rests solely in the color of their skin and the potency of their politics. The vision of Sacco and Vanzetti is built upon a politics of mercy and forgiveness that insists on feeding the hungry, clothing the naked, and sheltering the homeless. According to Vonnegut, such a politics poses a threat to a nation where greed controls the decision making of a capitalistic economy gone mad. Therefore, those like Sacco and Vanzetti are left with only their dignity as they bargain in good faith with a destiny that seems to hold only oppression, and it is their dignity that Vonnegut and Walter admire so much.[7] Out of respect for Sacco, Vonnegut uses as the epigraph to the novel Sacco's final letter to his thirteen-year-old son. In the letter, Sacco displays the faith in humanity that Vonnegut rediscovered at the end of *Breakfast of Champions*, and thus Sacco urges his son to care for the oppressed: "Help the weak ones that cry for help, help the prosecuted and the victim, because they are your better friends; they are the comrades that fight and fall as your father and Bartolo fought and fell yesterday for the conquest of the joy of freedom for all the poor workers. In this struggle of life you will find more love and you will be loved" (xxxix).

As we have seen elsewhere, Vonnegut, at all costs, wishes to fight against the exploitation of the poor, and, from his youthful memories of the Depression, he continues to believe faithfully and, perhaps, naively in the idealistic and pacifistic lessons taught to him by his junior civics teacher.[8] With the Sermon on the Mount in mind, Vonnegut comes bearing a message of consolation for those less fortunate, and, fittingly, he allows a man, dominated into submission by the narratives of greed and class, to tell this tale of redemption. As the narrator, Walter reflects on his fumbling progress from his inauspicious start as the son of immigrants to his years as a Harvard student and his eventual demise as a member of the Nixon administration. In *Jailbird*, Vonnegut gives to us a man who in his weakness unintentionally serves the narratives of greed and class only to be rescued by a narrative of compassion told to him by a shopping-bag lady. What makes Walter's tale so moving is the palpable guilt and sorrow evident in his description of an America moving ever closer to its doom. Walter fears the end of the America he has known in such people as Kenneth Whistler, the labor organizer, but he lacks the conviction to fight the injustices perpetrated by American government and its ruling class. As he says soon after bumping into Mary Kathleen O'Looney, shopping-bag lady and president of the most powerful corporation in the world, RAMJAC, "The most embarrassing thing to me about this autobiography, surely, is its unbroken chain of proofs that I was never a serious man. I have been in a lot of trouble over the years, but that was all accidental. Never have I risked my life, or even my comfort, in the service of mankind. Shame on me" (171). More to the point, Vonnegut seems to be saying, "Shame on us all!"

Walter's failings are the failings of all humanity because in Vonnegut's world we must accept the responsibility for such incidents as the Cuyahoga Massacre,[9] the deaths of Sacco and Vanzetti, the Nazi concentration camps, and the bombing of Hiroshima. Such events are central in Walter's moral universe because we all contribute to them. In our humanity we commit sins of omission and sins of commission. Vonnegut insists that no individual stands apart from the life of this world; no nation is removed from the ever-increasing threat of apocalyptic destruction. Quite simply, we are all in this together. Therefore, even though Walter commits no crime directly, he remains culpable as a member of the human race. But in the person of Mary Kathleen, the homeless angel who smells of trash and wears basketball shoes as big as skis, Walter is transformed. After being released from a federal prison in Georgia where he has served his sentence for the role he played in Watergate, Walter heads to New York City. What he rediscovers in the course of a few days in this sprawling metropolis are the ideals of his youth, namely, communism. As he explains, at one time in this country being a communist was so acceptable that it did not prevent him from winning a Rhodes Scholarship to Oxford after his graduation from Harvard, or, more to the political point, stop him from attaining a job in Roosevelt's Department of Agriculture. When Walter talks of communism, however, he attaches no

national boundary or political party to the idea. Rather, what he is
drawn to in communism is what Vonnegut is drawn to in Christ's
Beatitudes: compassion and common decency for all. In defense of
his communist ideas, Walter says,

> What could be so repulsive after all, during the Great Depres-
> sion, especially, and with yet another war for natural wealth and
> markets coming, in a young man's belief that each person could
> work as well as he or she was able, and should be rewarded, sick
> or well, young or old, brave or frightened, talented or imbecilic,
> according to his or her simple needs? How could anyone treat
> me as a person with a diseased mind if I thought that war need
> never come again—if only common people everywhere would
> take control of the planet's wealth, disband their national
> armies, and forget their national boundaries; if only they would
> think of themselves ever after as brothers and sisters, yes, and as
> mothers and fathers, too, and children of all other common peo-
> ple—everywhere. (13–14)

What Walter hopes for, against the soul-crushing force of the
modern world, is harmony among all peoples, and he acknowledges that the only way in which we will find such harmony is to
do away with the narratives of nationalism and wealth that are all
too often built upon misreadings of Christianity.

As is only natural in a novel by Vonnegut, in *Jailbird* we find
him subverting the narratives of nationalism and wealth while
offering some hope for the future in new readings of biblical texts.
Vonnegut, who speaks fondly of Christ but deplores the way so
many Christians have interpreted the Bible, says in a sermon he
delivered at St. Clement's Episcopal Church in 1980, "I am
enchanted by the Sermon on the Mount. Being merciful, it seems
to me, is the only good idea we have received so far" (*Palm Sunday* 325). But, as Vonnegut says in *Fates Worse Than Death*,
Christianity derailed when it stopped taking the Sermon on the
Mount seriously. According to Vonnegut, Christianity "was nothing but a poor people's religion, a servant's religion, a slave's religion, a woman's religion, a child's religion, and would have
remained such if it hadn't . . . joined forces with the vain and rich
and violent" (*Fates* 163). And so in *Jailbird*, Vonnegut lampoons
that kind of Christianity that has been propagated by the vain and
rich and violent when he satirizes Emil Larkin, a born-again

Christian serving time for his part in the Watergate conspiracy, whose constant attempts to save Walter from hell grow wearisome. What is most offensive to Walter about Larkin's preaching is his absurd devotion to eternal damnation. Fond of quoting from the book of Matthew in the New Testament, Larkin explains to Walter that Christ himself said, "Depart from me, you cursed, into the eternal fire prepared for the devil and his angels" (38). This biblical passage, Walter tells us, appalls him, and he is convinced that Larkin's devotion to such an idea explains the "notorious cruelty of Christians" (38).

Later in the novel, Vonnegut again points out the woeful errors found in the practices of modern Christianity by recounting a story written by Dr. Robert Fender, a veterinarian who was the only man convicted for treason in the Korean War. Fender is better known by his pen name, Kilgore Trout, and his story, "Asleep at the Switch," takes as its setting the pearly gates of paradise. It revolves around a group of heavenly auditors who decide whether a person deserves to enter heaven based solely on his or her financial success on earth. According to the auditors, each individual on Earth is given numerous opportunities for financial gain through the divine intervention of God's angels. If the auditor discovers that the individual has not taken advantage of these heavenly gifts, then that individual is reprimanded and told, "There you were, asleep at the switch again" (184). Needless to say, such theology grates on Vonnegut's social conscience, and in the character of Mary Kathleen he offers a more hopeful alternative to the capitalistic Christianity too often practiced by Americans in the last half of this century. Mary Kathleen, who devotes her life to others, has a grand dream to make Christ's Beatitudes a reality, and in Walter she sees the opportunity to flesh out her dream. Soon after their reunion, as Walter is being incarcerated by the police for the possible theft of clarinet parts, Mary Kathleen says to him with firm conviction, "I'll rescue you, Walter. Then we'll rescue the world together" (161).

Shortly before her untimely and accidental death, Mary Kathleen, as president of the RAMJAC Corporation, writes a letter making Walter a vice president in the financial giant that owns 19 percent of the United States. And, for a time, her dream does come true. Through Walter's influence and the posthumous wishes of Mary Kathleen, RAMJAC puts into practice the mercy and kindness Christ preaches in the Sermon on the Mount. But, of course, Vonnegut cannot accept so facile a solution to the grave problems we face, and soon Mary Kathleen's hope for a new paradise on Earth crumbles under the weight of governmental bureaucracy. Mary Kathleen's wish for RAMJAC, so closely aligned to Christ's Sermon on the Mount, can only fail in a world controlled by institutional machinery. In fact, as we are told, Mary Kathleen, like so many of the homeless and lost, is a product of the very economic and institutional machinery that eventually destroys her dream:

> Mary Kathleen O'Looney wasn't the only shopping-bag lady in the United States of America. There were tens of thousands of them in major cities throughout the country. Ragged regiments of them had been produced accidentally, and to no imaginable purpose, by the great engine of the economy. Another part of the machine was spitting out unrepentant murderers ten years old, and dope fiends and child batterers and many other bad things. People claimed to be investigating. Unspecified repairs were to be made at some future time. (140)

Like Christ, Mary Kathleen gives freely of herself and her fortune, and in her last will and testament she does not discriminate; rather, she gives without reservation all of RAMJAC's earnings and businesses to the American people in hopes of making those "unspecified repairs" that may empower the most needy. Like Christ's, however, Mary Kathleen's sacrifice is distorted by those in power. The government makes a mockery of her dream. Walter explains that after Mary Kathleen's will is discovered and the government gains control of her vast fortune, her dream of mercy and loving-kindness is destroyed quickly and remorselessly: "Foreigners and criminals and other endlessly greedy conglomerates were gobbling up RAMJAC. Mary Kathleen's legacy to the people was being converted to mountains of rapidly deteriorating currency, which were being squandered in turn on a huge new bureaucracy and on legal fees and consultants' fees, and on and on" (238).

Vonnegut, ever the realist, cannot end his work with Mary Kathleen's reverie for a peaceful economic revolution; the collapse of RAMJAC is inevitable given the nature of institutional workings. As in other Vonnegut novels, institutional machinery, created by humans but devoid of any human quality, represents our worst failings. And although Vonnegut longs for the mercy and kindness found in Christ's Beatitudes, he has lived too long to expect a miracle on such a grand scale. Therefore, at the close of *Jailbird*, turning away from any far-fetched fantasy of institutional salvation, Vonnegut embraces individual change in the person of Walter Starbuck. Because of the mercy shown to him by Mary Kathleen, Walter is transformed. No longer the man who merely mimics the proper emotional response, Walter truly believes in mercy and loving-kindness. The change in him is illustrated in an event recounted at a party thrown in his honor before he begins his new prison sentence for concealing Mary Kathleen's will. There, Walter listens to a recording of Congressional hearings where as a young man he had testified about his involvement and that of others with communism. When in the hearing Congressman Richard Nixon asks why Walter, a man who had benefited greatly from American capitalism, would involve himself with anything so vile, Walter replies simply, "Why? The Sermon on the Mount, sir" (241). So it is for Vonnegut. In the face of insurmountable evidence against us, he believes in the possibility of humanity's mercy and loving-kindness, offering hope in a postmodern age.

Deadeye Dick: Living in the Dark Ages

As we have seen in the course of his career, Vonnegut never rests easily in his guarded optimism. Although he continually strives to believe in humanity, his precarious position as a postmodern humanist is consistently threatened by humanity's incessant acts of deranged destruction. While *Jailbird* as a whole remains one of Vonnegut's more positive statements, his next two works, *Deadeye Dick* and *Galápagos*, journey deeply into the dark soul of a destructive world. Like *Mother Night*, *Deadeye Dick* struggles with the notion of innocence, and for Rudy Waltz, who accidentally kills a pregnant woman when he is only twelve years old, this struggle begins painfully in childhood and extends well into adult life. *Deadeye Dick* seems to ask, in an era when the vehicles of death proliferate at a frenzied pace and dispense their cargo of obliteration with what almost appears to be a mind of their own, to whom and for what are we responsible? Of course in his own darkly humorous way, Vonnegut crafts a tale that, while acknowledging the grave complexity of this question, cuts through it with graceful simplicity and ethical clarity.

In *Deadeye Dick*, as in other novels, in order to gain an ethical foothold with his readers, Vonnegut uses his personal history in an engaging manner. Drawing us into his own life by displaying the bright and the blemished equally for all to see, Vonnegut creates a bond of trust and security that few contemporary artists have achieved. The community of his readership affords him the opportunity to establish an ethical partnership. This partnership has become increasingly evident as Vonnegut grows in his desire to change with his words the moral nature of the contemporary world. We must not forget Vonnegut's declaration that "writers are the most important members of society, not just potentially but actually" (Allen, *Conversations* 166). Vonnegut believes fervently that as a writer he has a moral obligation to speak plainly about those ills that threaten the future of this planet and its inhabitants. During the early 1980s while Vonnegut was at work on *Deadeye Dick*, weaponry of all imaginable shapes and sizes rumbled off assembly lines to be shipped anywhere in the world to the highest bidder and used in innumerable games of death. The proliferation of this weaponry and the unbelievable advances in scientific technology that made possible its profoundly disturbing creation come together in *Deadeye Dick* as the author's worst nightmare: the neutron bomb. As many have argued, for Vonnegut the memory of Dresden offers only the unhallowed horror of desecrated humanity. But fifty years after Vonnegut had helped find corpses charred in the conflagration of incendiary bombs, we are threatened by a bomb that he considers far more heinous. The neutron bomb, death coiled tightly in its entrails, threatens to sweep down on black wings and embrace all living things on the Earth. Such a weapon, with its reverence for everything inanimate and its hostility for all things of the flesh, Vonnegut suggests in *Deadeye Dick*, must be deemed the ultimate enemy. In an interview, Vonnegut explains that our obsession with weapons of destruction is similar to the alcoholic's obsession with booze: "It seems to me the whole world is living like Alcoholics Anonymous now, which is one day at a time . . . , but there seems to be very little restraint in the world. . . . More weapons are manufactured every day and more arguments are gladly entered into and more enormous, dangerous lies are told. . . . We're totally warlike, and sooner or later something's going to go wrong" (Allen, *Conversations* 238–39). Therefore, for Vonnegut, the postmodern humanist who embraces all life, the neutron bomb represents, quite simply, the unholiest work

of the age. Within the neutron bomb, hidden with great care, is
what can only be described as our insane quest for self-annihilation; it is the logical outcome of the automated society found in
Player Piano and the prophetic beginning of a world similar to a
Tralfamadore, where the machines that fought the wars so effectively are the only survivors. Of course, the insanity of using
machines that destroy life while taking great care to preserve all
that is inanimate is not lost on Vonnegut. Thus, in *Deadeye Dick*
the author searches his past to understand how the world he lives
in has come to such an inhumane and irrational position.

Using bits and pieces of his own family's history to explore the
social fabric of America, Vonnegut recalls his father's fascination
with guns. As a youth growing up in Indianapolis, young Kurt,
much like Rudy, was given access to his father's most impressive
gun collection. As he tells us in *Fates Worse Than Death*, he and
his father were both members of the National Rifle Association, a
membership and a reading of the constitutional right to bear arms
that he has since rejected. Recently, in reaction to NRA television
commercials featuring the actor Charlton Heston, who praises the
group's good work, Vonnegut says, "I feel exactly as though he
were praising the germs of some loathsome disease, since guns in
civilian hands, whether accidentally or on purpose, kill so many of
us day after day" (*Fates* 81). As for the constitutional freedom to
bear arms, Vonnegut finds not Article II of the Bill of Rights
absurdly wrong but its current interpretation. Vonnegut actually
praises Article II and doesn't wish to change a word of it. What
upsets the author is the fact that gun advocates consistently forget
to include the introductory matter concerning a well-regulated
militia. As Vonnegut argues, "I only wish the NRA and its jelly-
fishy, well-paid supporters in legislatures both State and Federal
would be careful to recite the whole of it, and then tell us how a
heavily armed man, woman, or child, recruited by no official, led
by no official, given no goals by any official, motivated or
restrained only by his or her personality and perceptions of what
is going on, can be considered a member of a well-regulated militia" (*Fates* 81). Vonnegut can make no sense of the NRA's interpretation of the Bill of Rights, and his memories of his father's gun
collection and their time together using the weapons only convince him more that such foolishness is born of insecurity rather
than clear thinking.[10] The accusation that Vonnegut is a misanthrope is disproved by his desire to preserve and improve the

human condition. Far from misanthropic, Vonnegut's zealous crusade for gun control suggests a man who retains much of the idealistic energy of his youth. Vonnegut recalls that when he was a young man attending Shortridge High School in Indianapolis, the teachers often conducted an exercise requiring students to think of one way in which they planned to improve the world in their years to come. The teacher would ask the students to make a public promise to follow through on their idea. As a youth Vonnegut thought he would find a cure for some disease—a task requiring scientific training and equipment. But, today, Vonnegut says with his macabre humor, he does not "need an electron microscope to identify an AK–47 or an Uzi" (*Fates* 81).

Consequently, in *Deadeye Dick* Vonnegut magnifies the growth of weaponry in our culture and, with the razor sharp tip of his pen, begins to remove its cancerous growth. In an absurd parody of the many tragic deaths caused by the accidental discharge of guns that occur in America each day, Vonnegut constructs with great detail in the novel the events leading up to Rudy's lamentable firing of his father's Springfield .30–06. While *Deadeye Dick*, as a whole, does not at all times work within a plausible, realistic framework, Vonnegut appears to take special care to describe Rudy's initiation into the world of guns in a realistic manner. Vonnegut does not wish for anyone to claim that Rudy's use of guns is in some way unusual for a boy in America; such a claim would take away from the force of this postmodern morality play.

Telling his own story, Rudy explains that his father gives him the key to the family gun room on the day in 1944 when his brother leaves for active duty in the United States Army. The room holds a most impressive collection of modern and antique firearms that Rudy's father had first begun acquiring while studying art in Europe. Rudy refers to the gun room as the "Holy of Holies," and, at twelve years of age, he is shocked that his father chooses so soon to give him entrance to this prized and storied place in the adult world. After all, Rudy's older brother, Felix, had been fifteen before he was given the key that signified his passage into manhood. But especially fitting for such a decorous and ceremonial occasion, that morning at the Midland County Rod and Gun Club Rudy shoots far better than his brother and his father. Rudy describes these weekly outings to the club as "a Sunday-morning ritual" (52), and Vonnegut makes every effort to show how the men in the Waltz family replace religious devotion with devotion to weaponry. Vonnegut laments the Waltz family's decision to replace the comforting lies of church with those of killing machines; in an era of war, instead of listening to the church's message of love and peace, Rudy hears only the echoes of gunshot blasts at the Midland County Rod and Gun Club. By juxtaposing Rudy's passage into manhood with the war that his brother is leaving to fight in, Vonnegut calls attention to the sanctioned killing that "civilization" participates in on a regular basis. One of the freedoms that the war effort protects is the possession of firearms, and such a freedom, of course, continues to feed the cycle of violence. Because weaponry exists, humanity invariably uses it in order to enforce their claims to dominion over others. Without the tools of death, the tragic events that transpire in war could never take place. Without the freedom to bear arms, Rudy's tragic mistake would never have occurred. The Waltz family, of course, does not stand alone in its love of shooting. Rudy explains that "there were plenty of other fathers and sons, blazing away and blazing away" (52), and later Rudy discovers that his family is not even especially unique in terms of his shooting accident. Police Chief Morissey, who shot regularly with his son at the range, had in his own youth been responsible for the death of another man on a goose-hunting expedition when his ten-gauge shotgun discharged a foot from old August Gunther's head. Morissey's accident, however, received far less attention than Rudy's because the members of the hunting party, Rudy's father included, "in order to keep Morissey's life from being ruined by an accident that could have happened to anyone, launched Gunther's body for a voyage down Sugar Creek" (52). Vonnegut has Rudy tell the two stories of tragic shooting accidents together in order to introduce the question of Rudy's own innocence and our collective responsibility in such tragedies.

On the day Rudy receives the key, after lunching with his family and their distinguished visitor, Eleanor Roosevelt, he ascends the stairs to the gun room where his new privilege includes the duty of cleaning and storing those guns used that day. In a reverie about his newfound manhood and of admiration for his weapon, Rudy climbs with the Springfield, known for its stunning accuracy, into the cupola where he surveys the life of the town below. Writing his own story, Rudy describes the mutual affection between boy and gun: "So this was Mother's Day to most people, but to me it was the day during which, ready or not, I had been initiated into manhood. I had killed the chickens. Now I had been made master of all these guns and all this ammunition. It was something to savor. It was something to think about and I had the Springfield in my arms. It loved to be held. It was born to be held" (61). Even more, the Springfield, as any other gun, was made to be fired. And when Rudy does indeed fire it, he characterizes his mental state at that moment as "one with the universe" (63). In shooting the Springfield, Rudy experiences the transcendence for which so many search in religion, but unlike participation in religion, which Vonnegut often describes as harmlessly helpful, Rudy's new devotional produces a deadly force. As he discovers all too soon, on this Mother's Day his epiphany fosters not life, but death. When he fires the Springfield randomly into the air, Rudy murders a pregnant woman vacuuming on the second floor of her home eighteen blocks away, his bullet lodged square between her eyes. Thus in Midland City, because of Rudy's careless actions, he becomes known forever as Deadeye Dick.

The rest of Rudy's tale, quite simply, is one of retribution. But retribution, Vonnegut seems to suggest, should be the work of us all. In Vonnegut's fictional world, the tragedy of Rudy's action represents the sin of humanity, but like Mr. Metzger, the husband of the woman who has been killed by Rudy's bullet, Vonnegut does not condemn us. In Vonnegut's universe, forgiveness and mercy offer the best way through our travails. After all, we are new to the game of life, or, to use Vonnegut's own metaphor, our peepholes have been open for only the briefest of moments: What exactly can be expected of us?[11] Therefore, those mistakes that inevitably follow when someone new to the game bungles the pass must be forgiven, and in the game of life, which Vonnegut views as stacked unfairly against us, the best we can do is to comfort one another with respect and kindness. Of course, Vonnegut's game plan to bring respect and kindness to all involves the creation of a world devoid of the tools of destruction, a world of peace similar to the one in the novel Eleanor Roosevelt describes at Sunday dinner: "She said that there would be a wonderful new world when the war was won. Everybody who needed food or medicine would get it, and people could say anything they wanted, and could choose any religion that appealed to them. Leaders wouldn't dare to be unjust anymore, since all the other countries would gang up on them. For this reason, there could never be another Hitler. He would be squashed like a bug before he got very far" (59). But in the world where Rudy makes his lethal mistake, guns of all kinds do proliferate and peace exists only in the visionary songs of utopian dreamers. Consequently, Vonnegut does not hold Rudy as an individual entirely responsible for the errant bullet that claims Mrs. Metzger's life; rather, Vonnegut suggests that we are all in some way culpable for the crime. Because of our common condition, we must acknowledge the ways in which we affect one another for good or for ill. While it is true that Vonnegut finds it hard to create villains in his fictional world, this does not necessarily mean that Vonnegut does not believe in good and evil.[12] What Vonnegut insists we acknowledge is our interrelatedness, our interconnectedness. Lawrence Broer contends that Rudy's moral development culminates in his understanding "that the smallest acts of aggression are connected to the world's larger, bloodier deeds" (142). Without the devotion of Rudy's father to guns, Rudy would never have been given the opportunity to fire the rifle out the window. Without our culture's fascination with the weapons of death, Rudy's father would never have possessed such an arsenal. Without our culture's mores that deem artistic creation as effeminate and the discharge of guns as masculine, Rudy's father might never have experienced the insecurity that led to the purchase of his gun collection. The web of guilt and responsibility must cover us all.

Rudy's guilt about his own crime manifests itself in his devotion to his parents and in his future career as a pharmacist. As Rudy explains, "It was Deadeye Dick who was always trying to nourish back to health those he had injured so horribly" (130). But Rudy's penance does nothing to destroy the true root of such evil. Rudy's retribution at the local level offers a fine example of the kind of common decency of which Vonnegut speaks so often, but only the words of Mr. Metzger—Vonnegut's own voice lurking just beneath the surface—attack the actual source of the problem:

> My wife has been killed by a machine which should never have come into the hands of any human being. It is called a firearm. It makes the blackest of all human wishes come true at once, at a distance: that something die.
>
> There is evil for you.
>
> We cannot get rid of mankind's fleetingly wicked wishes. We can get rid of the machines that make them come true. I give you a holy word: DISARM. (87)

Such holiness represents Vonnegut's most sincere wishes, and those who call for an increase in arms and other lethal substances suffer the brunt of Vonnegut's wrath. As he said at an antinuclear rally in Washington on 6 May 1979: "We must now protect ourselves against our own government and our own industries. Not to do so would be suicide. We have discovered a brand-new method for committing suicide—family style, Reverend Jim Jones style, and by the millions. What is the method? To say nothing and do nothing about what some of our businessmen and military men are doing with the most unstable substances and the most persistent poisons to be found anywhere in the universe" (*Palm Sunday* 71). *Deadeye Dick* presents Vonnegut's plea for disarmament at the local and global level. In Rudy's tragic story, Vonnegut shows how individual actions ripple outward and scar the lives of so many in a community. But in the accidental detonation of a neutron bomb that obliterates all human life in Midland City, Vonnegut points to the danger of putting one's faith in institutions that have never shown concern for human life. Rudy suggests to us that the "accidental" detonation was no accident at all. Rather, he thinks that the government wished to test the new bomb and that Midland City offered a fine target " nobody cared about, where people weren't doing all that much with their lives anyhow, where businesses were going under or moving away" (234). Taking up placards to protest the devastating loss of human life, a group of farmers who call themselves "Farmers of Southwestern Ohio for Nuclear Sanity" claim that "the United States of America was now ruled, evidently, by a small clique of power brokers who believed that most Americans were so boring and ungifted and small time that they could be slain by the tens of thousands without inspiring any long-term regrets on the part of anyone" (231–32). While Vonnegut proceeds to poke fun at other conspiracy theories the farmers hold to be true, he does not belittle the notion that the government purposefully bombed Midland City. Because ideological metanarratives offered by governments have always been a target for Vonnegut, in *Deadeye Dick* he pleads with us to examine carefully the road down which they are leading us. In the end, Vonnegut insists, the simple faith we place in our supposedly "enlightened" institutions—institutions that are integral in the proliferation of all kinds of weapons—allow for untold atrocities. But, as Rudy says, "You want to know something? We are still in the Dark Ages. The Dark Ages—they haven't ended yet" (240).

Galápagos: A Pleasant Devolution?

For the three years following the publication of *Deadeye Dick*, Vonnegut continued to be consumed with the kinds of apocalyptic thoughts that permeated that novel. Of course, because of his experience at Dresden, his preoccupation with our potential destruction in a fiery cataclysm seems quite natural. Vonnegut's response to this threat in *Galápagos*, however, suggests an uneasy departure for the author. Rudy's estimation that we are indeed still living in the Dark Ages certainly expresses Vonnegut's own convictions about our current state of affairs. But the dramatic transformation of the human race that Vonnegut dreams up in *Galápagos* hints at the author's growing ambivalence about the importance of civilization. The tension between our idealized image of humanity's greatest achievements and the brutal reality of our destructive capabilities presents Vonnegut, as postmodern humanist, with an interesting dilemma: If the human race evolves into furry, seal-like creatures without "big brains"—as Vonnegut suggests we do in *Galápagos*—is it inevitable that in the ensuing edenic state humanity will lose everything that makes it so interesting; or, as the novel's ghostly narrator frequently asserts about what we have become after watching our transformation over a million-year period, "Nobody, surely, is going to write Beethoven's Ninth Symphony" (259). Not surprisingly, for Vonnegut the decision to alter humanity, even in his fictional universe, takes on a serious ethical dimension. As we have witnessed in previous novels, his desire to save the human race from itself runs strong and deep, but in wishing for our salvation are there boundaries that when crossed destroy the very thing that makes us most human? In this his eleventh novel, out of his devotion to humanity, Vonnegut acts as a postmodern prophet washed ashore to warn us of our potential destruction, but in his role as a prophet, he never loses the dark humor that has led so many to his work. There can be no mistaking the twinkle in his eye as he dreams of a world where our only ambition involves sunning ourselves on a bedrock made of lava until our hunger sends us diving for fish in clear, blue waters.

After completing *Deadeye Dick* and just prior to its release, Vonnegut journeyed with his second wife, the photographer Jill Krementz, to the Galápagos Islands for a vacation where he began to conceive of a world of peace, one in which humans might coexist with each other and other life forms without wreaking havoc on such a scale that the very existence of the world is threatened. As a humanist, Vonnegut wants very much for the human race to survive, but as a postmodernist, he acknowledges the precarious instability of humanity. As he explains in an interview:

> The most horrible hypocrisy or the most terrifying hypocrisy or the most tragic hypocrisy at the center of life, I think, which no one dares mention, is that human beings don't like life. Bertrand Russell skirted that, and many psychoanalysts have too, in talking about people lusting for death. But I think that at least half the people alive, and maybe nine-tenths of them, really do not like this ordeal at all. They pretend to like it some, to smile at strangers, and to get up each morning in order to survive, in order to somehow get through it. But life is, for most people, a very terrible ordeal. They would just as soon end it at any time. And I think that is more of a problem really than greed or machismo or anything like that. (Allen, *Conversations* 232)

With such thoughts in mind, then, in *Galápagos* Vonnegut conceives of a world where people can be satisfied with the most elemental, mammalian existence imaginable and where their capacity to harm each other or the planet is all but removed. In order to tell his tale in an effective and believable way, Vonnegut for the first time pays close attention to scientific detail in attempting to establish a note of authenticity. Unlike his other works of science fiction, *Galápagos* focuses more on defensible scientific theory and less on fanciful fictional constructs. Not only did Vonnegut explore the Galápagos Islands firsthand, he also spent many hours poring over the work of such noted scientists as Stephen Jay Gould and Carl Sagan. Allen goes so far as to say that the novel "often reads more like a textbook in evolutionary biology" than fiction (*Understanding* 149). Certainly sections of *Galápagos* resemble textbook materials, but we must never lose sight of the fact that Vonnegut uses such materials to explore what makes us most human. Vonnegut himself is proud of the scientific nature of *Galápagos* and explains in an interview that he received "a very nice letter from Stephen J. Gould who's the great zoologist at Harvard about this. He thought it was a wonderful *roman à clef* about evolutionary theory and also proves how random the selection is. He said that the fur-covered baby was a good mutation, that it was a common one. So it's reputable scientifically; I worried as much about that one as anything" (Allen, *Conversations* 252).

Armed with scientific knowledge, Vonnegut attempts to create an alternate reality in his fiction, a possible world of humane happiness that depends on a different moral order. Leonard Mustazza contends that since nature "is responsible for the organ that makes ethical evil possible, it accordingly falls to nature to correct its own mistake, in this case by radically remaking the human animal so that its form and priorities conform more with those of the rest of the mammalian kingdom" ("Darwinian Eden" 282). Mustazza's argument suggests that the ethical dilemmas we face are actually a product of our evolved brain structure. While Mustazza's response certainly may be supported by parts of *Galápagos*, Vonnegut is not entirely comfortable with such a notion. In fact, this matter belies any facile conclusion; the crux of the argument between the ethical dimension of human existence and the purely biological dimension of animal existence appears to generate the divisive energy that makes *Galápagos* such an interesting postmodern novel. In the end, it remains unclear whether in our devolution all that makes human life mysteriously liberating is lost, or whether our transformation into a creature without the mental capacity for ethical perturbation is far preferable to our current state of affairs.

In an interview with Allen, Vonnegut explains that "having seen where we're headed, I don't want to go that way anymore" (*Conversations* 292). Clearly, Vonnegut wishes to have nothing to do anymore with Vietnam Wars or Chernobyls or Three Mile Islands. He has seen enough of the atrocities created by human hands to realize that the complexity of human thought too often leads to our own destruction. Therefore, drawing on his trip to the Galápagos Islands, Vonnegut takes as his model for human happiness the life of the seals he sees playing joyfully and peacefully. Vonnegut explains that "if you saw the seals and sea lions on the Galápagos Islands, that's the life you would want. Gee, it's an incredible, amusing life they have. They play practical jokes on the other animals; they don't have that much to do. I mean, they're quite smart, and they've got a lot of time on their hands. Sharks are what they have to look out for—and killer whales" (Allen, *Conversations* 258). Against the backdrop of wars and murders carried out on a planet that has been effectively made unfit for so much mammalian life, including human beings, Vonnegut sees the life of seals as an unusually attractive option.

In order to build his case against humanity's current practices while holding out some small hope, Vonnegut gives to us in the course of the novel a group of characters who represent some of the worst evolutionary traits found in twentieth-century humanity, as well as some of the best; in the end, of course, devolution helps eradicate the worst traits while normalizing the best.[13] As Leon Trotsky Trout, the ghostly narrator of *Galápagos* and son of Kilgore Trout, explains, Jesús Ortiz is "Nature's experiment with admiration for the rich," and James Wait, a con artist who marries women only to steal their fortunes, is "Nature's experiment with purposeless greed," while Trout's mother is "Nature's experiment with optimism," and Akiko is "Nature's experiment with furriness" (82). Like Vonnegut, Leon says that the behavior of humans embarrasses him, and that "a million years later, I feel like apologizing for the human race" (82). What embarrasses Leon so much is our treatment of one another and the Earth. Recalling one of his father's science fiction novels, *The Era of Hopeful Monsters*, Leon briefly retells the story's basic plot. As usual, any story produced by Kilgore Trout's pen is nothing more than a sermon offered up by Vonnegut to turn us from our destructive and unethical ways, and in *The Era of Hopeful Monsters*, Vonnegut makes no attempt to veil the striking similarity between the dreadful demise of the world in the story and the current condition of the Earth:

> It was about a planet where the humanoids ignored their most serious survival problems until the last possible moment. And then with all the forests being killed and all the lakes being poisoned by acid rain, and all the groundwater made unpotable by industrial wastes and so on, the humanoids found themselves the parents of children with wings or antlers or fins, with a hundred eyes, with no eyes, with huge brains, with no brains and on and on. (82–83)

And so too in *Galápagos*, Vonnegut destroys the world not with a bang, but with the quiet dissolution of the human race by means of a virus that destroys the ovaries of all women on the planet. Only the group of castaways, isolated and forgotten on the Galápagos Islands, survives to propagate the human race. Slowly we witness the destruction of everything associated with the progress of civilization and the devolution of humanity into more simple creatures whose only desire is to swim and eat and mate. Repeatedly, Leon tells us that the only real villain in his story is "the oversize human brain" (270), and by the end of his tale this villain is unquestionably vanquished, posing no threat to the planet or the species.

But is this Eden? Mustazza contends that "the movement of the narrative is bidirectional, progressive in that it applies a Darwinian solution to the problem of moral error, retrogressive insofar as the state of innocence that is ultimately achieved is allusively linked to primal mythic innocence" ("Darwinian Eden" 279). Although it is true that Vonnegut, using Darwinian theory, solves the problem of moral error, in doing so he also destroys what makes us human. The primal mythic innocence of which Mustazza speaks also represents a state that appears inhuman in many respects. To return to the garden inevitably requires a transformation that abolishes sin and, as a consequence, all notions of morality. Without choice, human morality ceases to have meaning. Without our capacity for rational thought, many would argue, human life ceases all together. In an especially telling scene, Captain Adolf von Kleist, the captain of the *Bahía de Darwin* and the unsuspecting sire of the human race, throws into the sea the advanced computer, Mandarax. Leon describes von Kleist as a new Adam whose "final act was to cast the Apple of Knowledge into the deep blue sea" (62). Von Kleist's actions symbolize humanity's return to an edenic state where the fruit of knowledge, once eaten by Adam and Eve, is returned to its rightful place. The difficulty that Vonnegut, and in turn Leon, has with such a seemingly blissful condition can only be explained as incomprehension. Neither Vonnegut nor Leon can imagine how such a life can be fulfilling because the only condition any human knows is predicated on distinctions of wrong and right, sin and salvation, mortality and immortality. Quite simply, no human living or dead has experienced what we call life without the knowledge said to have entered mythically into this world with humanity's disobedience of God. To conceive of a condition in which this knowledge ceases to exist is effectively to stop being human.

Therefore, while Vonnegut struggles to find some way to save humanity, our devolution into seals does not satisfy him. At all times and often against his better judgment, Vonnegut remains an advocate of humankind. Certainly this is the view Leon takes in the end. For this reason, when Leon's father appears in the long blue tunnel leading to the afterlife, Leon does not succumb to his incessant ranting against the human race but instead chooses to stay and observe us for the next million years. Appalled that his son wishes anything to do with humanity, Leon's father says, "The more you learn about people, the more disgusted you'll become. I would have thought that your being sent by the wisest men in your country, supposedly, to fight a nearly endless, thankless, horrifying, and, finally, pointless war, would have given you sufficient insight into the nature of humanity to last you throughout all eternity!" (254). But for Leon even Vietnam cannot break his faith. Like his mother, Leon believes "that human beings are good animals, who will eventually solve all their problems and make earth into a Garden of Eden again" (257). The Garden of Eden that Leon and his mother hope for, however, allows for the beauty of artistic and intellectual creation, something that devolution cannot provide. Consequently, although Vonnegut creates a world that affirms Mr. Metzger's plea in *Deadeye Dick* that we disarm— as Leon points out, "Even if they found a grenade or a machine gun or a knife or whatever left over from olden times, how could they ever make use of it with just their flippers and their mouths?" (149)—he cannot find a way to allow for human creativity. With creativity comes the threat of human destructiveness, a thorny dilemma for which Vonnegut can find no resolution. Consequently, at novel's end we are left wondering which world is better: a world of the most base biological functions that poses no threat to life or a world of free will driven by an intellectual capacity that threatens humanity's very existence. Leon's response as he waits for the blue tunnel to appear again after one million years seems to sum up Vonnegut's own dissatisfaction with peaceful devolution: "I will of course skip into its mouth most gladly. Nothing ever happens around here anymore that I haven't seen or heard so many times before. Nobody, surely, is going to write Beethoven's Ninth Symphony—or tell a lie, or start a Third World War" (259). But even in his boredom, Leon must acknowledge the good that comes of humanity's innocent condition. Without the threat of a Third World War, he can say that his mother was right: "Even in the darkest times, there really was still hope for humankind" (259).

Finally then, *Galápagos* really solves nothing. Rather, like Jonathan Swift, Vonnegut satirizes our current condition with brutal honesty, but even though he has said in an interview that he cannot characterize the loss of human thought as a tragedy,[14] he certainly seems to agree with Leon that such a life offers only boredom, something that he might readily flee if a blue tunnel presented itself. *Galápagos*, if nothing else, remains a stern sermon filled with grave portent. In its delivery, however, Vonnegut, as postmodern preacher, never loses sight of the purpose behind the message: humanity. Consequently, regardless of its brooding darkness, it is only fitting that Vonnegut chooses the words of Anne Frank for the epigraph of *Galápagos*, because like Frank, Vonnegut remains a committed humanist who must say, "In spite of everything, I still believe people are really good at heart."

Bluebeard: Art and the Ethics of Redemption

After showing us where as a species we might be headed in *Galápagos*, in *Bluebeard* Vonnegut returns to the problem of how we treat one another on a daily basis in the contemporary world and what that treatment might suggest for our future on this planet. Appropriately, Vonnegut chooses for the epigraph of this novel the words of his son, Mark Vonnegut, MD, who said in a letter to his father, "We are here to help each other get through this thing, whatever it is." And whatever life is, Vonnegut faithfully and adamantly proclaims, it should entail caring for all humankind. In order to establish this golden rule, Vonnegut recognizes that he must in some way convince his readership that we are all interconnected, to one another and to the planet, that in some way we all have a stake in what the world becomes. Of course, Vonnegut is no politician or religious leader. The only tools he has to offer in this postmodern crusade to alter our course with destruction are his words, and, unlike Auden and other apolitical modernists, Vonnegut hopes to make something happen with his art. Like Rabo Karabekian in *Breakfast of Champions*, Vonnegut sets out in his art to show us the very thing that mystically infuses our experience: the awareness of the sacred in every living creature. Whether something sacred truly exists or is merely created with each stroke of Karabekian's brush or each word of some writer carries no weight for a postmodern humanist like Vonnegut. If the world can be apprehended only through language, then there remains no reason to struggle endlessly in order to prove conclusively that the human soul actually exists; rather, armed with this "comforting lie," Vonnegut may proceed in faith with the work of making this life, whatever it is, a better place for all concerned.

James R. Tunnell suggests that Vonnegut's body of work—as much a crusade to save humanity from itself as it is art—may be summed up in the form of a plea: "Don't let yourself adjust to the unthinkable and the unbearable. There's enough inhumanity in the world without adding to it. Be kind. Open up. Reach out. Have a heart" (133).

Bluebeard is the story of one man who has lost heart, a man who has for the most part turned his back to the postmodern landscape and settled in to wait for death. A victim of his past history, including the devastation of two World Wars, the Great Depression, the suicides of three close friends, a divorce, and the death of his second wife, Rabo Karabekian can find no reason to take part in the world of the living. But since *Bluebeard* is also a story of redemption, in this novel Vonnegut pays homage to the miracle of kindness and the beautiful rebirth that follows. For Rabo and the women who make his redemption possible, Vonnegut mixes his palette carefully in order to create his twelfth novel in a career that, spanning five decades, gives testimony to the undying faith of an artist who too often has been falsely accused of giving up on the human condition.

Bluebeard, which Allen characterizes as possessing "an extra measure of emotional warmth" (*Understanding* 159), focuses on the tension between art and life, and ultimately suggests that art can transform life, a claim that Vonnegut often makes. Since *Bluebeard* is essentially the spiritual and artistic autobiography of Rabo, we come to view the world and its sordid history through his one good eye. Moreover, in the process, we also come to understand the despair of this one-time abstract expressionist whose lifework has been destroyed because the paint he used, Sateen Dura-Luxe, despite its claim to "outlast the smile on the 'Mona Lisa,'" disintegrates completely. Left with nothing but empty canvases and long-dead friends and lovers, Rabo retreats from the world only to be rescued again and again by the kindness of women. And although *Bluebeard* intricately weaves its plot across the history of the twentieth century and spans two continents, the focal point of the narrative remains Rabo's soul. The health of Rabo's soul, as might be expected in a novel about an artist, is tied intimately to his moral understanding of painting.

Rabo's career as an artist begins—through the influence of his mother and Marilee Kemp, the mistress of illustrator Dan Gregory—when he leaves San Ignacio, California, to come to New

York City, where he hopes to become a great artist under Gregory's tutelage. An Armenian like Rabo's parents, Gregory illustrates for magazines in a fashion similar to that of N. C. Wyeth and Norman Rockwell. Gregory's uncanny ability to recreate in perfect detail any object or scene earns him the reputation of master realist, but it also showcases a moral flaw that leads to his eventual death. Like his paintings, Gregory sees the world in absolutes, completely and utterly indifferent to changing light and motion. He is an artist who captures life and reduces it in such a way that life ceases to be wondrous and mystical; in its place there is only the semblance of reality. Rabo explains that Gregory, in his guise as a painter, "was a taxidermist. He stuffed and mounted and varnished and mothproofed supposedly great moments, all of which turn out to be depressing" (84). Gregory controls with his art; he does not liberate, and without liberation and freedom the life force that imbues art is destroyed. Lawrence Broer contends that "Gregory's work is not just passionless, but dangerously reductionist—stagnant and morally simplistic. . . . Gregory, of course, is the 'lunatic' for portraying life in the form of human stereotypes and moral absolutes. His paintings, Rabo says, were truthful about material things, but they lied about the human spirit and the nature of reality" (164). By attempting to place the world perfectly onto his canvas, Gregory loses the nuances that make life rich in its possibilities; his inability to move beyond any facile understanding of ethical truth leaves him to create the kind of art that Vonnegut sees as most dangerous. Gregory is the artist of consummate skill who has no soul, and, fittingly, in the end he travels to Italy to join Mussolini's forces where his art becomes a tool for fascism.

While the work that Gregory gives Rabo to perform as his apprentice does eventually serve Rabo in his own artistic quest, it is the love he experiences with Marilee that truly transforms the young artist. Gregory gives to Rabo the same painting exercise that his own master had given to him: the perfect replication of his art studio, a room of astounding proportions and unusual artifacts. Rabo does indeed paint the studio in perfect detail, but each time he presents his work to the master it is summarily dismissed and tossed into the fireplace. Gregory finds fault with young Rabo's work because it has no soul, and, as Rabo explains, "I knew what he was complaining about, and the complaint wasn't laughable" (155). The complaint is exactly what Rabo fights against his entire life; like his painting, he stiffens with the effort to show others his soul, to share what lies deep within. The origin of this problem seems to stem from his parents' inability to show their love to their son. After their narrow escape from death in their own country during the genocide of the Armenian race, in Egypt Rabo's parents are swindled by a fellow Armenian who promises to place the couple in an Armenian community in California. Because no such community exists, together Rabo's parents slowly settle into a stupefying existence waiting for an end to this life. Five years before his father's death, Rabo and his father measure one another for suits from the Sears, Roebuck catalog on the occasion of Rabo's trip to the East. Rabo recollects that the event itself was surely unusual, but what was most strange was that the two men were required in the task to touch one another. Rabo explains, "I can't recall our ever having touched before" (73). Denied the physicality of love in his childhood, Rabo cannot express the very thing that makes our human condition worthwhile. Without love, platonic or erotic, Rabo cannot understand how to bring to life his artistic creations.

Therefore, although Rabo, as he puts it, goes to New York City "to be born again" (67), the surrogate father Rabo gains in the person of Gregory teaches him no more about love than his own parents. What is missing from his artistic father's paintings is the same thing missing from his biological father's life: an understanding that the human condition, at all times, must be fluid, filled with life and death and rebirth, not stasis. Rabo eventually perceives that Gregory's artistic vision is composed of nothing more than mindless replication. What Rabo wishes for so dearly in his own work is life, and he makes this claim clear when he defends the work of abstract expressionists[15] to Circe Berman, the writer who comes to live with Rabo late in life and in the process transforms him:

Let me put it yet another way: life, by definition, is never still. Where is it going? From birth to death, with no stops on the way. Even a picture of a bowl of pears on a checkered tablecloth is liquid, if laid on canvas by the brush of a master. Yes, and by some miracle I was surely never able to achieve as a painter, nor was Dan Gregory, but which was achieved by the best of the Abstract Expressionists, in the paintings which have greatness birth and death are always there. (84)

The first glimpse Rabo is given of such a world comes to him through Marilee. With Marilee's help, Rabo slowly begins to see the world of art as one where love may be shared, where life begins to take on its full shape. The secret liaisons between Marilee and Rabo in the Museum of Modern Art, a sacred place that Gregory forbids the two to visit, help Rabo to connect art with meaningful, soulful acts of faith. As Rabo explains to us, "Belief is nearly the whole of the Universe, whether based on truth or not" (152), and what Rabo discovers about his own art is that it does indeed lack a faith in the human soul. What Rabo longs to do is create a work of art that somehow acknowledges the pain and despair of this life while transcending it. He wishes to paint a picture that moves people beyond the darkness that any great painting must possess toward moments of hope and light. Of course, such a masterpiece cannot be painted by Rabo's hands until he learns from Marilee and so many others how to express such soulful actions in his own life.

With the example of her life, Marilee gives to Rabo his first lesson in selfless compassion. Marilee's actions, however, do not truly affect Rabo until much later in his life when, at Circe's request, he begins to write his autobiography. As Rabo uses language to explore his past, he comes to understand the debt he owes Marilee. What Marilee has done for Rabo is to treat him as no one else had: with love and respect. Not long after Rabo had been in New York City, he discovered that it was Marilee, not Gregory, all along who had corresponded with him and had sent art supplies through the mail. Unbeknownst to Gregory, Marilee had befriended Rabo, treating him as she wished she had been treated. Rabo later learns that when Gregory uncovered their secret friendship, he beat Marilee and threw her down a flight of stairs, breaking one arm and both her legs. Absurdly, Gregory seemed to be angered more by the loss of his art supplies and less with what he considered Marilee's infidelity with Rabo. Because of this loathsome incident, however, Gregory offers to grant Marilee any wish, and as a result Rabo comes to live in New York City. Never considering her own well-being, Marilee longs to see Rabo develop as an artist, and with her nurturing Rabo does indeed, despite Gregory's sadistic acts toward his apprentice, begin to understand what art can accomplish. In her love for Rabo, Marilee gives to us our first glimpse of a maternal nature that by novel's end will touch the lives of so many, inspiring Rabo's greatest artistic achievement.[16]

Marilee's kind actions bear an uncanny resemblance to another mother-figure in the fiction of John Irving who also attempts to heal those brutalized by the violence of this world. In *The World According to Garp*, Jenny Fields works diligently as a nurse to heal the psychic and physical wounds of all kinds of victims. Jenny, above all else, is a caregiver, the most ethical response Irving or Vonnegut can dream of in this world. Considering the friendship between Irving and Vonnegut, it should not surprise anyone that Marilee, like Jenny, attends to the needs of the damaged with such patient and loving kindness. Perhaps the most striking similarity between the two characters is the help they give to women damaged by the senseless acts of men. In Irving's novel, Jenny converts the estate at Dog's Head Harbor into a refuge for women. Among Jenny's wards are many victims of rape, in particular a group of women called the Ellen Jamesians who have cut out their tongues to protest the rape and mutilation of a young girl. In *Bluebeard*, after the end of the war in 1945, Marilee also establishes a home for women who have been victimized. Through a series of events, she marries the Count of Portomaggiore in Italy after Gregory's death and uses her position compassionately and benevolently to befriend the many women and children who are devastated by the fighting. When Rabo comes to visit her Italian estate after the war, she gives to him one more precious lesson about the nature of the world and its need for faithful compassion. In an extended story about one of the women she has befriended, Marilee explains to Rabo that the woman has lost a leg and an eye because of the soulless nature of men:

> Well, early one morning she crossed a meadow, carrying two precious eggs to a neighbor who had given birth to a baby the night before. She stepped on a mine. We don't know what army was responsible. We do know the sex. Only a male would design and bury a device that ingenious. . . . Women are so useless and unimaginative, aren't they? All they ever think of planting in the dirt is the seed of something beautiful or edible. The only missile they can ever think of throwing at anybody is a ball or a bridal bouquet. (224–25)

Though Rabo also loses an eye in the war, surprisingly, he remains unmindful of the far-reaching consequences of man's evil until Marilee's reprimand. Clearly, Marilee's story serves the same purpose as

Mary O'Hare's tirade against the cinematic representation of war in *Slaughterhouse-Five*. In his reflections on Gregory's art and the ethical strength of women like Marilee and Circe, Rabo, in the words of Lawrence Broer, comes to understand "the tendency of people to imitate art" (164) and the danger in such naiveté.[17] In an especially telling scene, Rabo recalls, "I can remember thinking that war was so horrible that, at last, thank goodness, nobody could ever be fooled by romantic pictures and fiction and history into marching to war again. Nowadays, of course you can buy a machine gun with a plastic bayonet for your little kid at the nearest toy boutique" (147).

Setting out to combat the nature of things nowadays, Rabo uses the only tool he has ever possessed—his skill as a painter. Thus he collects the blank canvases that once held one of his most ambitious abstract expressionist paintings, "Windsor Blue Number Seventeen," and begins to work secretly in the potato barn behind his home. Because "Windsor Blue Number Seventeen" was an eight-panel, sixty-four-foot painting named after the color of Sateen Dura-Luxe Rabo had used to create it, like all his other paintings, it too fell apart in time. After Rabo restretches and reprimes the canvases, he explains to his second wife, Edith, as they stand together before the pure white canvas landscape, that "this eccentric project was an exorcism of an unhappy past, a symbolic repairing of all the damage I had done to myself and others during my brief career as a painter" (275). What Rabo intends to do is leave the white canvases untouched. Thereby, he wishes to leave a world unblemished, one free of any injury perpetrated by human hands. In an act of confession, he thus gives the painting the title, "I Tried and Failed and Cleaned Up Afterwards, so It's *Your* Turn Now." But soon after his act of penance, Edith dies, leaving Rabo lost and bewildered. At her burial, Rabo has what he describes as his "strongest vision yet of human souls unencumbered, unembarrassed by their unruly meat" (277). Consequently, without hesitation he drives to a hardware store to buy art supplies, foregoing Edith's wake in the process. His beloved entered into the earth, Rabo seeks redemption for the unruly meat of humanity in the world of painting where, perhaps for a moment, our souls may be reborn unencumbered. Appropriately, his only word to the clerk at the hardware store is "Renaissance."

Inspired by his epiphany at Edith's funeral, Rabo does in fact experience a renaissance. He sees clearly for the first time the

nature of the work he must do and recognizes that the most crucial element he must supply is "soul, soul, soul" (277). At this
point in his life, however, Rabo finally finds the soul for which he
had long searched. Out of his pain, Rabo is reborn. His apprenticeship with Marilee, his time spent fighting in the war, the deaths
of his close friends, his failure as an artist, and the love he experiences with Edith—all have cultivated his soul in such a way that
now he may create a work of art transcending the otherworldly
nature of Terry Kitchen's abstract paintings and the cruelly reductionist nature of Dan Gregory's realistic illustrations. *Bluebeard*
ends with the unveiling of Rabo's highest achievement. Along with
Circe, the woman who has prodded and pushed Rabo to reveal his
soul to others, we witness the dazzling profundity of the sixty-
four-foot painting. Housed in the barn, the canvases fill what was
previously empty space with life and death and hope of redemption. What Rabo has painted is a scene that he witnessed at the
end of the war: a valley filled with concentration camp survivors
and prisoners of war and soldiers and farmers and lunatics set free
from asylums and the sun coming up over it all. Standing in the
middle of the painting, thirty-two feet of the picture extending out
on either side, Rabo describes what he has done:

> We were standing on the rim of a beautiful green valley in the
> springtime. By actual count, there were five thousand, two hun-
> dred and nineteen people on the rim with us or down below. The
> largest person was the size of a cigarette, and the smallest a fly-
> speck. There were farmhouses here and there, and the ruins of a
> medieval watchtower on the rim where we stood. The picture
> was so realistic that it might have been a photograph. (280–81)

Rabo stresses the painting's realism because there is a war story to
go with every figure. His painting defeats any romantic retelling of
war by emphasizing the life of each person before and after the
event that the picture actually chronicles. Because Rabo has finally
succeeded in bringing fluidity to his work, the canvas does indeed
hold birth and death and that which life offers between the two.

   While the painting is a culmination of the stories of all the survivors, it is also a new beginning. In the spring of 1945, walking
from among the corpses, those who still lived began again to
embrace one another, to help one another get through this thing
called life. Rabo's painting insists that we never forget the atrocities

committed by human hands, but it also insists that we remember only human hands can heal the injured and the sick and the dying. When Circe inquires about the title of the painting, Rabo quickly replies, "Now It's the Women's Turn" (286). As Rabo has learned, women offer the possibility of life.[18] He explains that for too long men have oppressed the very sex that might restore the planet. Because his own redemption would never have taken place without women, he says to Circe: "Twice now I've been a Lazarus. I died with Terry Kitchen, and Edith brought me back to life again. I died with dear Edith, and Circe Berman brought me back to life again" (299). On their walk back to the house, after looking at the paint- ing—Rabo calls it a "whatchamacallit" because it does what no other painting has attempted to do—Circe points out to Rabo that finally his "meat" has helped do something good for this world: "Well, then, isn't it time for your soul, which has been ashamed of your meat for so long, to thank your meat for finally doing some- thing wonderful?" (300). Rabo, indeed, does thank his meat, as we should also thank Vonnegut for doing something wonderful in the postmodern literary world: showing us the redemptive possibilities for the meat and soul of the human race.

Hocus Pocus: Weighing In at the End of the Century

Perhaps after the celebratory note upon which *Bluebeard* ends, we might expect a kinder, gentler work from the aging Vonnegut. Or, since Vonnegut has been compared so often to the great American humorist, Mark Twain, we might as easily expect in his later years a dark, acerbic turn against humanity. Vonnegut himself sees his career approaching an end. The truly prodigious body of work Vonnegut has produced prompts even him to write with mocking exasperation after his list of books in *Bluebeard*, "Enough! Enough!" Much to the delight of his admirers, however, Von- negut's body of work has not exhausted the vision that continues to fire our imaginations and that has encouraged many of his readers to commit to social and political action. Moreover, there is no sign that Vonnegut wishes to give up on humanity; if any- thing, Vonnegut appears only to have strengthened his resolve to make this world a better place for future generations. *Hocus Pocus*, published in 1990 when Vonnegut turned sixty-eight, attests to the energy that time and again drives the author to write novels he hopes may in some way transform this world; this same energy and conviction also keep Vonnegut on the road where he gives an endless number of speeches and, as he puts it, attempts to poison our minds with humanity (Allen, *Conversations* 123). In fact, during the early 1990s when *Hocus Pocus* first appeared, the United States witnessed a resurgence in activism unparalleled since the late 1960s and early 1970s. Not surprisingly, Vonnegut, who had been embraced by the counterculture twenty years before, once again found his work in vogue. *Hocus Pocus* sold briskly, made various best-seller lists, and drew favorable reviews from such writers as Jay McInerney and John Irving. Among some reviewers, however, the notion persists that Vonnegut subscribes to a fatalistic point of view, one similar to that of his Tralfamadorians. Certainly *Hocus Pocus*, the memoirs of Vietnam veteran Eugene Debs Hartke, contains much darkness, but the darkness is never portrayed as something to which we should succumb. Quite the contrary, Eugene's reminiscence is a moral account of his own life and that of his country. His tale, in the end, surely must be seen as one of Vonnegut's most emphatic statements against the ever-present darkness lurking within civilized humanity. Rather than accept defeat, *Hocus Pocus* calls attention to the rhetorical strategies, the "lethal hocus pocus," often used to justify our inhumane acts. In the novel's doing so, Vonnegut gives us fair warning about where our present course may lead us.

In a review of the book, John Leonard calls Vonnegut "a Johnny Appleseed of decencies" (Mustazza, *Critical Response* 305). Such a title is befitting an author who claims that "the mysteries which remain to be solved have to do with relating to each other" (Allen, *Conversations* 74). But in *Hocus Pocus*, Eugene reminds us that up until now we have come up woefully short of solving those mysteries. The future that Vonnegut dreams up in this novel is not as sensational as those in his earlier works. Eugene experiences no chrono-synclastic infundibula, nor does he journey to another galaxy. Actually, while the novel is set in the early twenty-first century, the incidents that take place in the novel have obvious precursors in our own time. The confessional tone of Eugene's story suggests Vonnegut's continued devotion to the kind of realism found in *Jailbird, Deadeye Dick*, and *Bluebeard*. Like Walter, Rudy, and Rabo, Eugene tells the story of his life in an attempt to make some sense of it all, to assuage the guilt of his country's and his own unethical and inhumane actions. The most

significant event in Eugene's life, the Vietnam War, remains the
single most traumatic event for our country in the last half of the
past century. Having written about the other major wars of the
twentieth century, Vonnegut finds it only natural finally to deal
with our actions in Vietnam. What Vonnegut describes in Eugene's
narrative is the fulfillment of humanity's darkest wishes in the
nightmarish technology used during the Vietnam War. In his
vision of the twenty-first century, Vonnegut contends that if we do
not learn to respect one another despite the color of our skin or
the level of our education or the God we believe in, then quite
soon we too will be living in postapocalyptic times where crime
runs rampant and the Earth's days are numbered. As Eugene
explains, "At least the World will end, an event anticipated with
great joy by many. It will end very soon" (13). But Eugene and
Vonnegut are not among those who anticipate this world's demise
with great joy. Unlike numerous religious groups, they possess no
faith that expectantly awaits the return of some deity who will create a new Heaven and Earth. What Eugene and Vonnegut do possess is a vision of a world made better by our own humane efforts.
Rather than rejoice at the end times, Eugene writes with passion-
ate grief about our loss of compassion for one another.

Eugene's memoirs, edited by "K.V.," are written on tiny scraps
of paper pieced together as a collage. Like Howard Campbell, at the
time Eugene writes the book, he is a prisoner, waiting to be tried for
a crime against the state. Eugene is charged with instigating the
prison break in Scipio, New York, where he had been a teacher after
his dismissal from his first teaching job at Tarkington College across
the lake. Although Eugene did not help in the prison break, he
nonetheless believes he is guilty of other crimes and, perhaps,
deserves some form of punishment. The charge against Eugene is
racist in nature: the legal officials believe that only Eugene, a white
man, could have masterminded such an escape in an all-black
prison. The truth of the matter is that some of Eugene's most
humane actions occur while he teaches at the prison, but helping
organize a prison break is not among them. For the first time, at the
prison Eugene helps others with no clear reward in sight; because of
Eugene several inmates learn to read and write and are eventually
awarded their high school diplomas. But in the completely segre-
gated prison system of the future, Eugene inevitably becomes the
scapegoat. As he looks back over his life while he waits to stand
trial, he begins to evaluate his actions, specifically the number of

women he has made love to and the number of people he has killed
as a military man. Much to his surprise, the number on the two lists
is the same. As Eugene explains to his attorney, he wishes to be
buried with his two lists so that on the Judgment Day he may say
to the Judge, "Judge, I have found a way to save you some precious
time in Eternity. You don't have to look me up in the Book in Which
All Things Are Recorded. Here's a list of my worst sins. Send me
straight to Hell, and no argument" (*Hocus* 150). Eugene's lawyer
responds as might be expected; he believes that with the two lists—
scrawled so sloppily with Eugene's ravings about sin—they will
have no trouble winning a plea of insanity.

. Of course, his lawyer's response is exactly what Eugene is
attempting to expose in his memoirs. Our inability to recognize
unethical or immoral acts frightens Eugene. That is not to say
Eugene's morality is reductionist or simplistic; he certainly sees the
relative nature of many ethical problems, including his consistently adulterous behavior.[19] He cannot, however, see any way to
justify morally what was played out in Vietnam. As Eugene says,

> What a relief it was, somehow, to have somebody else confirm
> what I had come to suspect toward the end of the Vietnam War,
> and particularly after I saw the head of a human being pillowed
> in the spilled guts of a water buffalo on the edge of a Cambo-
> dian village, that Humanity is going somewhere really nice was
> a myth for children under 6 years old, like the Tooth Fairy and
> the Easter Bunny and Santa Claus. (194)

Eugene wishes no rhetorical games to be played on his behalf; he
knows all too well the slippery nature of language and how to use
it to cover up the most awful dealings humans can imagine. Therefore, he says to his lawyer, "But the lists aren't based on halluci-
nations. I'm not getting them from a radio set the CIA or the fly-
ing-saucer people put in my skull while I was sleeping. It all really
happened" (150). Evidently, Eugene believes, as does his creator,
that actions that destroy human life are, quite simply, wrong, and
our loss of the critical faculty that makes it possible to identify
immoral or unethical behavior presents the most horrifying implications for the future yet. Lies told to further the destruction of
this planet or its people are to be loathed.

And so Eugene loathes his past. As an officer in Vietnam,
Eugene tells us, he was responsible for innumerable deaths of

Americans and Vietnamese alike, including some women and children. Most of the deaths, however, do not result from Eugene calling in an air-strike or tossing a grenade or firing a gun; rather, his weapon of choice was language:

> In Vietnam, though, I really was the mastermind. Yes, and that still bothers me. During my last year there, when my ammunition was language instead of bullets, I invented justifications for all the killing and dying we were doing which impressed even me! I was a genius of lethal hocus pocus!
>
> You want to know how I used to begin my speeches to fresh troops who hadn't yet been fed into the meat grinder? I squared my shoulders and threw out my chest so they could see all my ribbons, and I roared through a bullhorn, "Men, I want you to listen, and to listen good!"
>
> And they did, they did. (148)

Vonnegut has stressed his entire career the formidable power of language to shape our notion of reality. Time and again he has pleaded with his readers to use language to comfort one another. Philosophical inquiries into the truth of our existence, according to Vonnegut, are futile exercises. What we should spend our time doing is composing constructive, comforting lies that end wars and poverty and racism. If we wish to use hocus pocus, we must use it responsibly for the good not only of ourselves but of others. Such thoughts echo in *Hocus Pocus* as Vonnegut's grandfather's words surface once again. Eugene tells us that his grandfather believed, as do the German freethinkers of Vonnegut's Indianapolis youth, "that nothing but sleep awaited good and evil persons alike in the Afterlife, that science had proved all organized religions to be baloney, that God was unknowable, and that the greatest use a person could make of his or her lifetime was to improve the quality of life for all in his or her community" (175–76). Such are Eugene's dreams of a world of peace, and, in his own way, Eugene does what he can to make such a world come true. By working first at a college for special-needs students and then at a prison for black inmates who have been abused by a system that sees them as mere cogs in a flesh-eating machine, Eugene does penance for his tragic past. He does what he can to improve the quality of life at Tarkington College and the prison. But in the end he meets defeat at the hands of people who are "about 1,000 times dumber and meaner than they think they are" (55).

The Board of Trustees at Tarkington College finds Eugene's teaching un-American and dismisses him because he dares speak of the good in Karl Marx's prescription for an ideal society: "'From each according to his abilities, to each according to his needs'" (96), an idea that struck Eugene's grandfather as "sounding like the Sermon on the Mount" (97). Lawrence Broer contends that Eugene nurtures moral responsibility by telling his story (179). Eugene's bildungsroman, not surprisingly, leads him to live in the spirit of his namesake, Eugene Victor Debs, whose words serve as the book's epigraph: "While there is a lower class I am in it. While there is a criminal element I am of it. While there is a soul in prison I am not free." Hartke's memoirs suggest that empathy leads to postmodern righteousness, not judgment. *Hocus Pocus* counters those who believe they have the right to make those judgments that Eugene believes should be reserved for God, if God does indeed exist. For Eugene, the Sermon on the Mount seems to be the best lie we have been given to get through this life. Eugene's autobiography asks implicitly how anyone can live comfortably knowing that people starve to death daily, that nations constantly steal from indigenous peoples in the name of Providence, that right now our government spends millions of dollars to build machines that can destroy the very ground we stand upon. Judging by the way we live, Vonnegut suggests that we may think a bit too much of ourselves. Like Vonnegut, Wendell Berry, who has devoted much of his life to educating the masses about their relationship to this world, argues in *The Unforeseen Wilderness* that in "the woods we come face to face with the creation, of which we must begin to see ourselves a part—a much less imposing part than we thought" (66). Like Berry, Vonnegut suggests that we must learn to see ourselves as connected to one another and to the physical world; if we destroy one life or one part of this planet, then we harm ourselves. As Eugene concludes, "Just because some of us can read and write and do a little math, that doesn't mean we deserve to conquer the Universe" (302).

Timequake: Vonnegut's Gift to the Future

As Vonnegut resides in the early part of the twenty-first century— a place in time in which he set *Timequake*, the novel he struggled with for much of the 1990s—he continues to be active, speaking out against nuclear arms and poverty, against the war on terror and the problems facing the Middle East. *Timequake*, which originally was scheduled for release in the fall of 1993, was finally published in 1997. In the foreword to *The Vonnegut Encyclopedia* in 1994, Vonnegut remarked that the novel might never be finished: "I have been unable to complete it to my own satisfaction, so perhaps it will never be" (ix). In the prologue to the novel, he explains that during the winter of 1996 he found himself "the creator of a novel which did not work, which had no point, which had never wanted to be written in the first place" (xi–xii). As so often happens to his own characters, despite his best intentions, Vonnegut found himself failing. Like Billy Pilgrim in *Slaughterhouse-Five*, Vonnegut the author and Vonnegut the character were coming unstuck in time—but to no apparent benefit for his failing novel or for the world beyond the pages of the novel. The writing wasn't coming together, nothing was being changed for the good, and, as usual, the world looked like a damned mess to this postmodern harlequin from the Midwest.

Thankfully, Vonnegut found a metaphor in Ernest Hemingway's experience with *The Old Man and the Sea* that helped him to continue swimming toward the novel's conclusion and eventual publication. Having suffered harsh reviews from critics for his novel *Across the River and into the Trees*, Hemingway wrote a tale of perseverance about an older fisherman who would not give up his catch, regardless of the damage the sharks did to it. In similar fashion, Vonnegut tells us that he "had spent nearly a decade on that ungrateful fish (*Timequake*)" and that "it wasn't fit for shark chum" (xii). What was the author to do? Vonnegut's answer: "Fillet the fish. Throw the rest away" (xii). Thus, what we have in Vonnegut's last novel—to this date Vonnegut stubbornly says he will not write another one—is a failure of sorts. Like *Slaughterhouse-Five*, which Vonnegut tells us fails as a novel—a comment that he makes in terms of the traditional, generic ideas about what a novel ought to do—*Timequake* also fails in terms of generic unity as it struggles with the nature of time and what we might learn from our understanding of how we pass through time.

Vonnegut's final novel is the quintessential postmodern pastiche. The book might best be seen formally as the culmination of a career that hinted at such radical dissolution of the conventional novel or memoir and that Vonnegut finally produced in his eighth decade. *Timequake* glues together portions of a memoir with fic-

tional characters from a failed novel, several plot outlines struggling with the demands of the writer in his "reality" outside the
text, and numerous anecdotes from a career of writing that never
found a home in any other book. *Timequake* presents the reader
with a published novel within a memoir within a failed, unpub-
lished novel within a sociological tract (replete with strong admonitions about ways to live ethically), and, of course, this odd amal-
gamation is punctuated by joke after joke. Vonnegut's premise, for
what he professes will be his final novel, fits seamlessly with the
rest of his canon: A timequake strikes on 13 February 2001 trans-
porting everyone back to 17 February 1991. This glitch in time,
however, does not allow us to undo the wrongs we may have committed the first time we lived through the years from 1991 to
2001. No, in Vonnegut's universe, which is Kilgore Trout's universe as well, we are all consigned to experience the exact same
actions, the exact same decisions, until the timequake brings us
back to 13 February 2001, at which time free will is restored. "We
all had to get back to 2001 the hard way," Vonnegut explains,
"minute by minute, hour by hour, year by year, betting on the
wrong horse again, marrying the wrong person again, getting the
clap again. You name it!" (xiii).

Like Billy Pilgrim coming unstuck in time, Vonnegut plays
with the big ideas of free will and predestination. He includes the
graduation address he gave at Butler University in Indianapolis,
Indiana, to highlight these very issues. In the address, Vonnegut
explains that he, like Robert Pinsky who did the same at a poetry
reading Vonnegut attended, ought to apologize for the fact that he
has lived a much nicer life than normal.

> If I had it to do all over, I would choose to be born again in
> a hospital in Indianapolis. I would choose to spend my child-
> hood again at 4365 North Illinois Street, about ten blocks from
> here, and to again be a product of that city's public schools.
>
> I would again take courses in bacteriology and qualitative
> analysis in the summer school of Butler University.
>
> It was all here for me, just as it has all been for you, the best
> and the worst of Western Civilization, if you cared to pay atten-
> tion: music, finance, government, architecture, law and sculp-
> ture and painting, history and medicine and athletics and every
> sort of science, and books, books, books, and teachers and role
> models.

People so smart you can't believe it, and people so dumb
you can't believe it. People so nice you can't believe it, and people so mean you can't believe it. (11–12)

In this address, Vonnegut acknowledges that his life is in part
what it is because of chance, because he happened to be born in
1922 to the Vonnegut family in Indianapolis, Indiana. As in *Palm
Sunday*, he reflects upon the role the Midwest played in shaping
his worldview, and how he never really left home. As his characters travel through the timequake, chance (which for Vonnegut
blurs with certain ideas about predestination) controls their circumstances. There is nothing they can do to change the outcome
of their lives or deaths. It already has been determined by history,
by the passage of time, and no amount of effort will allow them
to alter one bit of it. Free will is a thing of the past, so to speak.
In this way, *Timequake* echoes Vonnegut's previous work in novels like *Slaughterhouse-Five*.

But another impulse imbedded in Vonnegut's philosophy,
the one that preaches action despite, or perhaps because of, the
circumstances of one's birth, begins to play within the borders
of this constructed universe as the timequake passes. "In real
life, as during a rerun following a timequake," Vonnegut
explains, "people don't change, don't learn anything from their
mistakes, and don't apologize" (139), and upon the return to
the present, Kilgore Trout is the only person in Vonnegut's
novel that understands free will has once more kicked in. Catastrophe after catastrophe occurs as people who have run their
lives on automatic pilot for the past ten years continue to act as
if they need only go through the motions. What a fabulous
metaphor Vonnegut has created. Indeed, so much of what has
destroyed our planet and its inhabitants might be deemed the
result of a species that cannot or will not turn off the automatic
pilot. As Trout runs to wake the world from its automatic slum-
ber, he returns to one of Vonnegut's main proposals for a postmodern world where a new kind of humanism might flourish
and make a difference: extended families. And as he so often
does, Vonnegut's first move amidst chaos is toward practicality.
He looks at the structures we already have in place and asks
what might be done with them. His proposal: add the following
articles to the Bill of Rights.

Article XXX: Every person, upon reaching a statutory age of puberty, shall be declared an adult in a solemn public ritual, during which he or she must welcome his or her new responsibilities in the community, and their attendant dignities.

Article XXXI: Every effort shall be made to make every person feel that he or she will be sorely missed when he or she is gone. (175)

"Such essential elements in an ideal diet for a human spirit, of course," Vonnegut remarks, "can be provided convincingly only by extended families" (175). This idea already serves as the basis for *Slapstick,* and throughout *Timequake* Vonnegut returns to the questions and provisional answers that populate his previous works. The grand questions that give him pause as he passes through the world are once again on display, and once again it is clear that while Vonnegut has passed into his eighth decade, he has not lost the unrequited love for the mystery of living.

The final Kilgore Trout story, which served as the original ending to the original "failed" *Timequake,* seems representative of so much we would call Vonnegutian. In this scene, Trout is ready to retire to his bedroom for the evening. Vonnegut as a character in his own book stands next to him. The two look to the stars as Trout comments on the expanding universe and the new quality of human awareness that resides there. "Your awareness," Trout explains. "That is a new quality in the Universe, which exists only because there are human beings. Physicists must from now on, when pondering the secrets of the Cosmos, factor in not only energy and matter and time, but something very new and beautiful, which is *human awareness*" (213–14). Upon further reflection, Trout revises this term and says, "Let us call it *soul*" (214). In this way, Trout and Vonnegut remind us that our awareness of the universe and all it holds is a sacred trust, that despite our struggles with it, it is worth our faith. Thus, Vonnegut's major contribution to American literature rests firmly in his gift of a postmodern humanism, in his ability to affirm *human awareness,* or what Kilgore Trout renames *the soul,* despite the dark chaos he chronicles. In an age that too often tenders only the shibboleths of inhumanity and evil, Vonnegut continually gives us examples of how to get on with the business of life, a business that he insists must be filled with kindness and compassion.

After examining the breadth of Vonnegut's constructed world, it is clear that he writes from a position similar to that of Henry Giroux, who has argued convincingly that there can be "no tradition or story that can speak with authority and certainty for all of humanity" (465). Moreover, this position, Klinkowitz claims in *Structuring the Void*, results from Vonnegut's anthropological training, which, as was noted earlier, "convinced him that reality was something arbitrary and impermanent, since the basic facts of life could be changed by circumstances of birth or by the whims of national economics even after one was half-grown" (37). Such an understanding of the postmodern condition allows Vonnegut to create the sorts of fiction that help expose the constructed and decentered nature of our world. This step is only the initial gesture toward Vonnegut's philosophical position. Ultimately what concerns Vonnegut most is our response to the postmodern condition. The central question for Vonnegut remains, What does one do in a decentered world?

For Vonnegut, the fact that we can know our world only through language, through the fictions we create, does not make the plight of humanity any less real. Through several thousand years of civilization, the physical and spiritual needs of men and women continue to be pretty much the same. Thus, Vonnegut shows great concern for those people who have been oppressed and degraded by the grand narratives of modernism in America. Yet for Vonnegut there is still hope. Because we may create our own narratives, the petites histoires of which Jean-François Lyotard speaks, the possibilities for personal as well as societal change are endless. As Klinkowitz explains, "If reality is indeed relative and arbitrary, then it is all the easier to change; men and women need not suffer an unhappy destiny, but can instead invent a new one better suited to their needs" (*Structuring* 37).

As we have seen in the course of this study, in much of Vonnegut's writing, there is attempt after attempt to retell old, but useful, stories. Moving through the Western tradition with abandon, Vonnegut uses sources as divergent as Christ's Sermon on the Mount and the philosophical writings of his great-grandfather, German freethinker Clemens Vonnegut. Unconcerned with the sanctity of tradition, Vonnegut wishes to recreate fictions to better serve our needs, an activity that, according to Zygmunt Bauman, requires "nerves of steel." Bauman argues that postmodernity has a new determination "to guard the conditions in which all stories can be told and retold, and again told differently" (23). In the retelling, however, there can be no dogmatism, no reestablishment of a fixed center. It is, as Bauman suggests, "living with ambivalence," a frightening prospect for a culture moving away from a traditional narrative of rationality and objectivity based upon a fixed center of reference. As Bauman claims, the work of postmodern humanism does, indeed, require nerves of steel. Vonnegut, however, appears to be just the writer for the job.

Consequently, as we face the daunting task of improving the human condition, Douglas Kellner suggests we need both modern and postmodern theory to understand the ways in which positive, redemptive work may be accomplished. Kellner hopes to find some way to fuse the freedom of postmodern thought with a modern value system that insists on the sanctity of human life. Having grown to manhood during the modern age, Vonnegut embraces an ethical code that reveres human life. But having blossomed as an artist during the early years of the postmodern age, Vonnegut cannot accept the essentialism of the system of morality with which he was raised and on which the system stands. In Vonnegut, Kellner finds the writer who can at once expose the charade of essentialism while telling a story that offers a postmodern humanism concerned with the oppression of all people and their freedom to tell their own stories. For this reason, Vonnegut is a vocal defender of the First Amendment. He is concerned at all times with our freedom and ability to tell our own stories because he believes that in their telling we can begin to understand the ways in which we all affect what this world will become. Of course, Vonnegut does recognize the danger in the proliferation of those narratives that lead to the destruction of life. In his own lifetime, he has witnessed the heinous abuses created by the narratives of such storytellers as Hitler and Jim Jones, whose "comforting lies" exploited the very worst traits in humankind. Thus, Vonnegut hopes to lead others to tell stories that redeem our existence, that construct better realities for the oppressed and the privileged alike. Considering Vonnegut's claim that the human brain is a "two-bit computer" designed to "make up comforting lies," it is not surprising that each of his thirteen novels forces the reader to examine the world's current state of affairs while suggesting alternative ways of living.

What makes Vonnegut different from many other postmodernists is his refusal to accept complete relativism. He emphatically asserts a single rule for our comforting lies: "Ye shall respect one another" (*Fates* 159). This rule is one that appears in a slightly different form in Vonnegut's early fiction, when Eliot Rosewater, rehearsing what he will say at the baptism of Mary Moody's twins, exclaims, "God damn it, you've got to be kind" (*God Bless You* 110). In *Fates Worse Than Death*, Vonnegut explains that he likes to think that Jesus said in Aramaic, "Ye shall respect one another," "something almost anybody in reasonable mental health can do day after day, year in and year out, come one, come all, to everyone's clear benefit" (159–60). Vonnegut confesses that his single rule for postmodern living is based entirely on a leap of faith. The postmodern morality that runs through Vonnegut's fictional world presupposes that human life is valuable, and it does so with no possible way to substantiate its claim. Nonetheless, Vonnegut stands by this claim. Despite the mounting evidence against the human race, Vonnegut continues to believe in the very fiction he has himself created. At the center of postmodern humanism is the assertion that life is precious and that every attempt should be made to improve the condition of our planet in order to preserve life.

Vonnegut appears to be an anomaly in the postmodern age. He is the writer who works fervently to save a planet and its inhabitants from what many claim is a certain doom. He is a social prophet who tells his stories in hopes that words can in some way change the dark reality of the present age. In Vonnegut's response to the conundrum of the postmodern condition, there lies a gift for the future: the possibility for each of us to touch the lives of others with kindness and common decency.

Notes

1. Postmodern (Midwestern) Morality:
The Act of Affirming Humanity in a Screwed-up World

1. As Jerome Klinkowitz contends in *Literary Disruptions: The Making of a Post-Contemporary American Fiction*, Vonnegut is "probably the most talked-about American novelist since Ernest Hemingway" (33). In 1975, when Klinkowitz made this statement, he explained that in virtually every bookstore, prominently displayed, hung a poster of Vonnegut "peering across the list of books he has written" (33). This same poster, like portraits of W. B. Yeats in Irish pubs, according to Klinkowitz, also could be found in many bars and pizzerias on college campuses. Since the 1970s, at the height of Vonnegut's fame, there has been a decline in the value of Kurt Vonnegut as pop icon, but this decline has not been as complete as Merrill depicts.

During the 1980s, Vonnegut was visible in film and on campuses across the nation. In the comedy *Back to School*, Vonnegut writes a research paper about himself for Rodney Dangerfield, a paper that the professor returns with a failing grade and the explanation that whoever has written the paper knows nothing about the author; in addition to this film appearance, the cable network Showtime invited Vonnegut to host the series *Kurt Vonnegut's Monkey House* based on his short stories, while the University of South Carolina captured numerous interviews with the author on video tape. Off camera, Vonnegut continues to speak on the lecture circuit, drawing crowds of thousands, and remains a best-selling author with sales in the millions. Adding to his pop-culture fame, each year the television program, *Entertainment Tonight*, celebrates his birthday with other celebrities born on November 11, flashing his image to homes across the nation. Away from the glitter of television, during the 1990s Vonnegut was a marketing fixture for the Barnes and Noble chain of bookstores, who sold his likeness on coffee mugs, T-shirts, and book bags, while using him in their advertising campaigns as well. Vonnegut also participated in the advertising and marketing plans of such companies as Absolut Vodka, offering them an original drawing that refers to *Cat's Cradle*. Such evidence certainly suggests the strength not only of Vonnegut's writing but his public persona as well.

2. At this point, I wish to acknowledge the invaluable service William Rodney Allen has performed for Vonnegut scholars; his work compiling and editing *Conversations with Kurt Vonnegut* has produced a volume that accurately portrays the development of Vonnegut's public persona and contains the most representative and significant interviews to date.

3. For the best discussion of Vonnegut's college writing, see Robert Scholes's "Chasing a Lone Eagle: Vonnegut's College Writing," collected in *The Vonnegut Statement*.

4. To date, only a small number of book critics have mentioned Vonnegut's desire to enact social change, and even fewer academic critics have examined Vonnegut's moral posturing. In 1988, Merlin Snider completed a dissertation at the University of Southern California entitled "Morals and Irreligion: Kurt Vonnegut as Social Ethicist"; the premise of Snider's research is promising but its emphasis fails to move away from binary assumptions and modernist rhetoric concerning moral and aesthetic value. Surprisingly, no critic has yet tried to discuss Vonnegut's attempts to establish a postmodern position that accounts for the pragmatic need to make moral decisions, to do work that positively affects social problems such as poverty or racism or sexism, while facing the issue of a decentered and fragmented universe, one that seems not to allow for essentialist or absolutist moralities.

5. In a review of Vonnegut's novel *Hocus Pocus*, the novelist Jay McInerney calls Vonnegut "the leading literary big-question asker."

6. Early in Vonnegut's second novel, *The Sirens of Titan*, Malachi Constant naively proclaims, "I guess somebody up there likes me" (7). In this novel and elsewhere, Vonnegut not only struggles with the existence of God but more importantly with the possibility of divine intervention. While this theological problem haunts Vonnegut, it does not take precedence over what he sees as our obligation to each other, an obligation that requires daily activity. Malachi Constant, in the end, realizes that "a purpose of human life, no matter who is controlling it, is to love whoever is around to be loved" (313).

7. As Vonnegut has revealed in several essays, interviews, and speeches, members of his family have had bouts of depression—and understandably so when one looks at the events of his parents' losses during the Depression, or Vonnegut's own loss of his mother to suicide, his sister Alice to cancer, and her husband to a train accident twenty-four hours after the death of Alice—and that these have led to the treatment of family members by the medical community. Perhaps the most significant incident shaping Vonnegut's thinking about mental illness concerned his son, Mark Vonnegut. Now a pediatrician at Massachusetts General Hospital, Mark was once diagnosed as schizophrenic and treated with vitamin therapy. The doctors who helped Mark to recover were among the first to suggest that mental illness was not entirely psychological and that chemical imbalances in the body affected behavior. This experience is recounted in Mark's book *The Eden Express*, and the notion of chemical composition controlling human behavior, at least in part, has found its way into Vonnegut's own novels, as is the case in *Breakfast of Champions*. Kurt Vonnegut continues to give speeches and write essays about mental illness and his family's experiences with the medical profession: a speech he delivered to the Mental Health Association in 1980 is included in *Palm Sunday* (238–43), and an introduction to a new edition of *The Eden Express*, as well as an essay he wrote after reading an anthology of poems and short prose by persons in institutions for the mentally ill, are collected in *Fates Worse Than Death* (205–9 and 235–37). The most significant study of Vonnegut's work in this context is Lawrence R. Broer's *Sanity Plea: Schizophrenia in the Novels of Kurt Vonnegut*.

8. Vonnegut's response to his trip to Biafra was not suicide, but tears. He recounts his return to Manhattan, where he checked in to the Royalton Hotel (his family was skiing in Vermont): "I found myself crying so hard I was barking like a dog. I didn't come close to doing that after World War II" (*Fates* 174). Experiences like Biafra or Mozambique, quite obviously, play a part in the author's consistent plea that we respect one another, an action that must involve our participation in meeting the needs of the global community.

9. As I speak about Vonnegut's moralizing, both in his books and during interviews and speeches, I do not mean to give the impression that he sees himself as a guru who through his wise teachings may save the world. On the contrary, he continues to be self-deprecating, using irony to undercut any pomposity. He describes this speech parenthetically as a time when "I was nutty enough to believe that I might change the course of history a tiny bit" (*Fates* 117) and concludes by telling us that the speech received polite applause, but "What a flop!" (120).

10. Vonnegut's fictional world is populated with scientists who naively use their talents only to have their inventions exploited for purposes of war, for the destruction of human life. In *Cat's Cradle* we meet the father of the atomic bomb, Felix Hoenikker, whose final gift to the world is ice-nine, a substance that in the end destroys life as we know it. These characters, with great irony, insist on the purity of science and inevitably are proven wrong as their pure pursuits turn against humanity.

11. Vonnegut is an avowed atheist who sporadically attends a Unitarian Church. A self-proclaimed freethinker and German idealist, he continues to examine religion, especially Christianity, finding many of its tenets attractive. In *Palm Sunday*, Vonnegut describes himself as a "Christ-worshipping agnostic," and it is interesting to note that this atheistic freethinker has incorporated several Christian principles into his own philosophy, going so far as to retell the orthodox Christian story of Christ's birth in his only children's book, *Sun Moon Star*.

12. A fine example of such evidence is found in Vonnegut's speech to the graduating class of 1974 at Hobart and William Smith Colleges, where he succinctly asserts his position: "For two-thirds of my life I have been a pessimist. I am astonished to find myself an optimist now. I feel now that I have been underestimating the intelligence and resourcefulness of man" (209).

13. Vonnegut, whose writing is often compared to Mark Twain's, speaks glowingly of Twain in many speeches and interviews; in fact, he named his firstborn son, Mark, after Twain. Of particular interest is the speech he delivered in 1979 on the one hundredth anniversary of the completion of Twain's home in Hartford, Connecticut, a speech later collected in *Palm Sunday*. In this speech, Vonnegut claims that Twain, in *A Connecticut Yankee in King Arthur's Court*, has effectively and with great irony skewered the chief premise of Western civilization, a premise that impels the Yankee and his band of workers to their horrific entrapment by death; the premise, Vonnegut suggests, continues to dominate our culture and increasingly other world civilizations. He explains the premise in this manner: "the sanest, most likable persons, employing superior technology, will enforce sanity throughout the world" (171). Obviously this sanctioned "sanity" appears all too insane to the likes of Twain and Vonnegut.

14. Two of the most accessible studies of the relationship between modernism and postmodernism are Rosenau's *Postmodernism and the Social Sciences* and Steven Best and Douglas Kellner's *Postmodern The-*

ory: Critical Interrogations. Rosenau's book attempts to divide the debate over what postmodernism means and what the implications are for this meaning into two camps: skeptical postmodernism and affirmative postmodernism. Although this sort of binary paradigm might lead to results that are reductive, Rosenau somehow manages to represent the complexity and wide range of diversity inherent in these differing positions. Best and Kellner cover an enormous range of seminal postmodern texts, outlining their major tenets while offering some insight into their nuanced complexity. Best and Kellner are clearly affirmative postmodernists, but their critical project does not accept postmodernity wholesale.

15. Linda Hutcheon, in *A Poetics of Postmodernism: History, Theory, Fiction,* claims that "Texts could conceivably work to dismantle meaning and the unified humanist subject in the name of right-wing irrationalism as easily as left-wing defamiliarizing critique: think of the works of Celine, Pound, and others (whose politics tend to get ignored by the French theorists who prize their radical form)" (183). This is problematic for those who wish to embrace the positive political action of postmodernism. If postmodernism has no shared center of value, then the possibility for abuse by fascists or racists remains open, and such groups, of course, establish conditions that Lyotard, among others, would find intolerable. The question remains: How does one make judgments and apply those judgments to other communities beyond the local? As postmodernists, can we attack those practices we deem inhumane outside of the locality that established the values by which we could make such judgments, or are we relegated to attending to our own communities?

16. It is reasonable to say that the work of Jacques Derrida and Paul de Man, among other poststructuralist philosophers, reconfigured literary studies as has no other theoretical project in the past half century. Whether one agrees with their theoretical position is not at issue; it is clear that a great deal of the profession situates itself in relation to deconstructive principles.

17. In *The Transparency of Evil,* Jean Baudrillard argues that "by annihilating [evil's] own natural referents, by whitewashing violence . . . , by performing cosmetic surgery on the negative" (81), we have made it impossible to recognize the ways in which evil moves and infiltrates. In an effort to examine the nature of evil in contemporary culture and the astonishing success of those who wield it, Baudrillard uses the Ayatollah Khomeini's horrifying regime and more specifically his death threat against Salman Rushdie as fitting examples of the kinds of evil postmod-

ern culture may produce. I argue that the success of "evil" in contemporary culture is due in large part to our naiveté about the power of deconstruction and other postmodern discourse; while the proliferation of multiplicities is exceedingly important, it is not a panacea. We need to
recognize that the social efficacy of postmodernity's theoretical systems
may have limits in the material world.

18. At present, the debate over essentialism continues in multiculturalist, feminist, and post-colonial studies. The historical tendency of
Women's Studies or African-American Studies, among others, has been to
essentialize difference, to champion biological or spiritual essence that
some argue first led to the marginalization of minorities by Western
European culture. The insistence by some critics on an essentialist point
of view may be directly related to the history of oppression these groups
have endured. During the brutal and horrific oppression of African
Americans in the United States, for example, the kinds of coping strategies used by this people to sustain themselves physically and emotionally
may be characterized as spiritual in nature; this devotion to spirit and an
emphasis on essential difference remains a strong force in a large part of
the African-American social and political community. A change, however, is occurring as African-American and feminist scholars confront the
radical assertions of poststructuralism. Critics like Cornell West or Jane
Flax examine the implications of the poststructuralist critique as it relates
to the political power of the marginalized and the potential social benefits it may offer. Some critics, however, suggest that the recent turn away
from essentialism is merely a postmodern tactic of oppression, limiting
groups of people who, by proclaiming the essential difference of their
race or culture, had only just begun to make inroads against social domination. I contend that the most fruitful criticism, as it relates to Hassan's
shibboleths and our desire to move toward wholeness and a regeneration
of the human condition, is occurring in certain branches of feminist and
multiculturalist studies.

19. I do not mean to suggest that postmodernism has not affected
our daily practices in profound ways. Rather, at this point in time, I argue
that few people actually move outside of the purview of the modernist
subject; instead, as Kellner suggests, we appear to be caught between
modernism and postmodernism, living in both dispensations. Moreover,
considering the historical impetus behind the idea of an essential, individual subject, it would be uncanny if in a matter of decades such a fun-
damental transformation occurred decisively or peremptorily. The very
nature of our language, the manner in which we fashion the subject in

NOTES TO CHAPTER 1

our texts and in our speech patterns, problematizes the potential for such a radical change. Therefore, although postmodernism continues to establish new ways of looking at the world, ways that positively influence our treatment of the postmodern subject, our notion of that subject (outside of the theoretical) remains, for the most part, essentialist.

20. Interestingly enough, in spite of postmodern theory's insistence that the subject is not an essence, that the idea of a unified self is highly erroneous, we have witnessed in the past thirty years the "me" generation, self-help programs of all kinds, and psychotherapy that prods us toward self-actualization or what some refer to as a connection with our inner child. The popular culture of the postmodern age appears to be especially concerned with the individual self.

21. Vonnegut continually deconstructs the idea that all problems may be solved, that humanity, using the tool of science or religion, can somehow create a utopia. As he explains in an interview with *Playboy*, "it strikes me as gruesome and comical that in our culture we have an expectation that a man can always solve his problems. There is that implication that if you just have a little more energy, a little more fight, the problem can always be solved. This is so untrue that it makes me want to cry—or laugh" (Allen, *Conversations* 91).

22. Since Gardner's *On Moral Fiction* appeared in 1978, many other critics have entered the debate over the viability and profitability of ethical criticism. Perhaps surprisingly, one of the most vocal advocates of ethical criticism is J. Hillis Miller. In *The Ethics of Reading* and *Versions of Pygmalion*, Miller examines the ethical nature of reading from a deconstructive position, arguing that what is ethical or moral cannot be understood or confronted directly: "Storytelling is the impurity which is necessary in any discourse about the moral law as such. . . . There is no theory of ethics, no theory of the moral law . . . without storytelling" (*Ethics* 23). The range of critics who work in the field of ethical or moral criticism is indeed diverse, and, as such, it comes as no surprise to find such divergent theoretical ideas being produced in a discipline that has heretofore been neglected and now yields forth a truly important harvest. A critic of note in the field of ethical criticism is Terrence Des Pres who, like Elie Wiesel, the writer he most admires, concentrates on the efforts of certain artists, especially Jewish writers, who use their craft as a means of protest and therapy against the tragic and heinous events of the Holocaust. Other critics who are rethinking and recreating the field of ethical criticism include Frederick J. Antczak, whose work focuses on the ethical

nature of rhetoric; Martha C. Nussbaum, whose study centers itself on moral philosophy and uses literature selectively to better understand "real life" ethical conundrums; Susan Resneck Parr, whose research deals exclusively with the effects of ethical criticism on secondary education classroom practices; and Christopher Clausen, whose writing follows the more traditional patterns of literary study as practiced by Wayne Booth, among others. For an overview of the theoretical arguments and debates, as well as examples of the practice of ethical criticism, see Todd F. Davis and Kenneth Womack's *Mapping the Ethical Turn*. Certainly, it is clear that ethical criticism has been renewed, marking a significant addition to literary studies.

23. Martha Nussbaum explains that when she first began to investigate the relationship between ethical study and literary study, she "rarely found anything but contempt for ethical criticism of literature" (13). Ironically, the academy, in its attempts to combat the negative effects of ethical criticism, namely censorship, found itself censoring academic freedom. Such censoring most certainly led to the loss of many profitable readings. Ironically, although New Critics attempted to argue that art in some fashion transcends the ethical or moral, they actually were participating in a system of valuation that was itself ethical. Postmodern critics argue that the new critical claim to transcendence is an impossibility, unattainable in this world because of the nature of existence: all acts are ethical and political.

2. Searching for Answers in the Early Novels: Or, What Are We Here for Anyway?

1. As other critics have pointed out, Vonnegut's science fiction is dystopian in nature. Throughout his career he has worked diligently to undermine the notion that the "truth" of science will save us, that the destruction of our planet is of no concern because technology will take us to other worlds. In a book like *Galápagos*, Vonnegut offers a future world where technology has destroyed the earth as we know it, and humanity has evolved to a "better" state: people have smaller brains and the bodies of seals.

2. Although I argue that Vonnegut merely flirts with the notion of a return to an earthly paradise, Leonard Mustazza, in *Forever Pursuing Genesis: The Myth of Eden in the Novels of Kurt Vonnegut*, has written an extensive study arguing the importance of this theme in all of the novels up to and including *Bluebeard*.

3. Vonnegut's experience at the Hopefield School appears to have provoked the writer concerning the issues of difference and equality. In the short story "Harrison Bergeron," as well as toward the end of *The Sirens of Titan*, Vonnegut playfully creates a society that tries to nullify any special skills or talents that its members may possess in an attempt to make the least talented and the most talented individuals equal.

4. Jane Vonnegut Yarmolinsky recounts the tragic events leading to the adoption of Alice's children in *Angels without Wings*. While she substitutes names in this memoir, the correlation between the events and the historical persons involved is unmistakably clear.

5. Rumfoord's description of time as a roller coaster draws heavily on the Tralfamadorian notion of time. The idea that time is not linear contributes significantly to Malachi's understanding of the universe; without a beginning and an end, the need for meaning and purpose and a sense of causality appears to be negligible. Tralfamadorian concepts will continue to play a major role in Vonnegut's fiction, especially *Slaughterhouse-Five*.

6. Bruce J. Friedman, in his book *Black Humor*, explains that a characteristic of American writing involves finding humor in the bleakest moments. Vonnegut has responded to this label by explaining that "Freud had already written about gallows humor, which is middle-European humor. It's people laughing in the middle of political helplessness. . . . It's humor about weak, intelligent people in hopeless situations. And I have customarily written about people who felt there wasn't much they could do about their situations" (Allen, *Conversations* 90–91).

7. Richard Giannone, in *Vonnegut: A Preface to His Novels*, develops his reading of *Cat's Cradle* by focusing on the archetypes of Jonah and Ishmael. Vonnegut consistently uses such archetypes to emphasize our inability to understand how the universe functions. Malachi Constant in *The Sirens of Titan* is the precursor to the Jonah we find in *Cat's Cradle*.

8. In an interview, Vonnegut explains that anthropology has colored his writing in numerous ways: "It confirmed my atheism, which was the faith of my fathers anyway. Religions were exhibited and studied as the Rube Goldberg inventions I'd always thought they were. We weren't allowed to find one culture superior to any other. We caught hell if we mentioned races much. It was highly idealistic" (Allen, *Conversations* 181). The relativism stressed in the discipline of anthropology remains crucial to Vonnegut's conception of truth and narrative.

9. Extended, artificial families play a crucial role in Vonnegut's fiction. Often such an idea of family is held out as utopia, but, of course, Vonnegut at some point subverts any notion of utopia. Still, Redfield's theories and Vonnegut's imaginative perseverance eventually culminate in *Slapstick* when Eliza and Wilbur Swain develop the theory of artificially extended families. Wilbur institutes such a policy when he is elected president, and, as his campaign buttons proclaim, people never need be lonesome again.

10. William L. Godshalk has written an impressive detailed analysis of the intertextual nature of *God Bless You, Mr. Rosewater* and *Hamlet* entitled "Vonnegut and Shakespeare: Rosewater at Elsinore."

11. Klinkowitz and many others point to the fact that Trout is a character who pays dubious homage to Vonnegut's own career as a writer of science fiction. In *God Bless You, Mr. Rosewater*, Trout becomes the mouthpiece for Vonnegut's admonitions late in the novel. The kinds of moralistic statements that Trout proclaims in defense of Eliot's actions are nearly identical to statements Vonnegut has made on numerous occasions in interviews and speeches. Klinkowitz suggests that Vonnegut "came the closest ever to being Trout himself" during the time he was writing *God Bless You, Mr. Rosewater* (*Vonnegut Statement* 20).

12. Paul Fussell has written two excellent books examining the social and cultural impact of World Wars I and II: *The Great War and Modern Memory* and *Wartime: Understanding and Behavior in the Second World War*. Many of the ideas I present about the psychological horrors veterans faced as they attempted to reenter society are based on Fussell's work.

13. In an address at Bennington College in 1970, Vonnegut implored the students to understand the nature of scientific truth, not to blindly put their faith in the inventions of humanity. Vonnegut explains in a moving recollection the loss he felt when the narrative of science failed him, shattering his optimistic dreams:

> I thought scientists were going to find out exactly how every thing worked and then make it work better. I fully expected that by the time I was twenty-one, some scientists, maybe my brother, would have taken a color photograph of God Almighty and sold it to *Popular Mechanics* magazine. What actually happened when I was twenty-one was that we dropped scientific truth on Hiroshima. (*Wampeters* 161)

14. Schriber examines Vonnegut's work using the novel tradition as a guide. She argues that "the novel tradition hovers over *Cat's Cradle* and other Vonnegut novels as well precisely because it is called up and then cast out" (283).

3. Apocalyptic Grumbling: Postmodern Righteousness in the Late Novels

1. While Vonnegut did little with the dramatic arts after 1972 until the 1990s when Showtime began to film *Kurt Vonnegut's Monkey House*, from 1970 to 1972 there was a flurry of theatrical activity connected with his work. Besides the theatrical production of *Happy Birthday, Wanda June*, there is also the excellent film version of *Slaughterhouse-Five* directed by George Roy Hill, the National Educational Television production of *Between Time and Timbuktu or Prometheus–5* (an amalgam of excerpts from Vonnegut's novels and stories), and a dreadful film production of *Happy Birthday, Wanda June*. Although it appeared in the early 1970s that Vonnegut would devote himself exclusively to drama, the following remarks concerning film suggest one possible reason for his quick exit from and his subsequent return to the writing of novels: "The worst thing about film, from my point of view, is that it cripples illusions which I have encouraged people to create in their heads. . . . Well, so much for film as compared with print. As a friend said of another terrific theory of mine: 'It has everything but originality'" (*Between Time and Timbuktu* xv–xvi).

2. Vonnegut is forever tormented by his own mother's suicide, and the possibility that he will someday also be the victim of mental illness plays an important role in much of his art. In an interview that took place soon after the publication of *Breakfast of Champions*, he speaks hopefully about moving beyond the spectre of suicide: "*Breakfast of Champions* isn't a threat to commit suicide, incidentally. It's my promise that I'm beyond that now. Which is something for me. I used to think of it as a perfectly reasonable way to avoid delivering a lecture, to avoid a deadline, to not pay a bill, to not go to a cocktail party" (Allen, *Conversations* 109). Sadly, Vonnegut did attempt suicide in 1984, but since that time he once again appears to be embracing life. The state of the world deeply disturbs Vonnegut, and his writing continues to be his best form of therapy, a positive way to save himself, if not the world, from self-destruction.

3. Vonnegut's work has long been the subject of censorship, and he has, at times, defended his work in print. The most interesting case involves the banning of *Slaughterhouse-Five* by a school board in Drake, North Dakota. In "Kurt Vonnegut on Censorship and Moral Values," Richard Ziegfeld reprints Vonnegut's letter to the school board. Ziegfeld claims that Vonnegut's argument may be broken down into three segments: "that he is (1) a real person whose feelings have been hurt; (2) that he is a good citizen; and (3) that his work is not pernicious" (633). As might be expected, Vonnegut does not allow the school board to dehumanize him; he adamantly asserts his humanity, moving out from beneath the faceless name that graces the cover of the book. Unfortunately, even Vonnegut's unique and humane defense of his work has not deterred a variety of ideological groups from censoring several of his novels.

4. While Vonnegut remains a strong, vocal advocate of the First Amendment, he does acknowledge the abuses of this freedom by the pornography industry. Vonnegut's objection to pornography, however, is not based on some Puritan sensibility that causes him to blush at the sight of human flesh; rather, his disgust results from the appropriation of human flesh by the machinery of photography with no concern for what makes us most human. For Vonnegut, pornography remains simply human plumbing: the machine without the soul. In a telling comment, Vonnegut explains the difference: "My books are being thrown out of school libraries all over the country—because they're supposedly obscene. I've seen letters to small town newspapers that put *Slaughterhouse-Five* in the same class with *Deep Throat* and *Hustler* magazine. How could anybody masturbate to *Slaughterhouse-Five*?" (Allen, *Conversations* 186). For the most complete discussion of these issues, see the first chapter of *Palm Sunday* and the seventh chapter of *Fates Worse Than Death*, where Vonnegut writes exclusively about the First Amendment and the precarious nature of such legislation.

5. As discussed earlier, the anthropological theories of Dr. Robert Redfield affect Vonnegut's thinking in dramatic ways. In *Palm Sunday*, Vonnegut explains that "when I went to the University of Chicago, and I heard the head of the Department of Anthropology, Robert Redfield, lecture on the folk society, which was essentially a stable, isolated extended family, he did not have to tell me how nice that could be" (116), and Vonnegut remains committed to the project of providing such structures to America in *Fates Worse Than Death*. In a speech to the American Psychiatric Association, collected in *Fates Worse Than Death*, Vonnegut

says, "All of you, I am sure, when writing a prescription for mildly depressed patients, people nowhere as sick as my mother or my son were, have had a thought on this order: 'I am so sorry to have to put you on the outside of a pill. I would give anything if I could put you inside the big, warm life-support system of an extended family instead'" (35). Vonnegut realizes, however, that such a life-support system has its own flaws, and in the preface to *Wampeters, Foma & Granfalloons*, he acknowledges that such schemes are indeed utopian in nature (xxiv). Whether or not the return of extended families is plausible, they remain a comforting lie that Vonnegut refuses to renounce. As he says in response to an interviewer who asks whether Vonnegut has researched the plausibility of his scheme: "No. I'm afraid to. I might find out it wasn't true. It's a sunny little dream I have of a happier mankind. I couldn't survive my own pessimism if I didn't have some kind of sunny little dream. That's mine, and don't tell me I'm wrong" (Allen, *Conversations* 80).

6. When pressed about his ideas, Vonnegut explains that in an artificial extended family relatives would still act in much the same manner as they do today; the significant difference would be in the number of relatives: "If they asked for too much, he could tell them to go screw, just the way he would a blood relative. And there would be ads and articles in the family monthly about crooks or deadbeats in the family. The joy of it would be that nobody would feel alone and anybody who needed seven dollars until next Tuesday or a babysitter for an hour or a trip to the hospital could get it" (Allen, *Conversations* 84).

7. We are told in the first lines of chapter 20 that "Sacco and Vanzetti never lost their dignity—never cracked up. Walter F. Starbuck finally did" (*Jailbird* 182). Like Hemingway, Vonnegut also establishes a code of sorts. Vonnegut's code insists upon mercy, which he explains "is the only good idea we have received so far" (*Palm Sunday* 325), and dignity, which he describes succinctly as "Bargaining in good faith with destiny" (*Slapstick* 2). Vonnegut eulogizes the deaths of Sacco and Vanzetti because in the face of injustice and certain death, they asked only for the merciful treatment of humanity with grace and solemnity.

8. Vonnegut continually surprises himself with his innocent faith in humanity, but he never does so without poking fun at his own sentimentality, at his own idealism. In *Jailbird*, Walter says that his idealism did not die in the Nixon White House or in prison or in his new role as vice president of the Down Home Records Division of The RAMJAC Corporation. Of his faith in such idealism, Walter concludes, "I am a fool" (14). Like Walter, Vonnegut acknowledges the foolishness of some of his ideas,

but such ideas, he argues, are no more foolish than those that have led to so much death and destruction. In fact, the merciful faith Vonnegut places in humanity, while nonsensical in light of our crimes, offers the possibilities of beauty and goodness to a world desperately in need of such hope.

9. It should be noted that the Cuyahoga Massacre, which transpires on the grounds of the Cuyahoga Bridge and Iron Company, is a fictional event. Vonnegut states clearly that this confrontation between strikers and police and soldiers "is an invention, a mosaic composed of bits taken from tales of many such riots in not such olden times" (xxi).

10. Vonnegut suggests that his own father's fascination with guns reflected the insecurity he felt as an architect. Vonnegut explains that when he was a boy there was a homosexual panic in Indianapolis and that men who did not work at jobs like running a steam laundry and selling cars were targets of homophobic harassment: "And my father was right on the edge of the woman's world as an architect. His father had been in the same spot. So they'd collect guns and go hunting with the best of them" (Allen, *Conversations* 275).

11. In an interview, Vonnegut defends himself against the accusation that he is a misanthrope. Far from condemning humanity, Vonnegut explains, "My real feeling is that human beings are too good for life. They've been put in the wrong place with the wrong things to do" (Allen, *Conversations* 226).

12. In the preface to *Happy Birthday, Wanda June*, Vonnegut reveals that one of the last things his father said to him before he died "was that I had never written a story with a villain in it" (ix). Although Vonnegut does not often create villainous characters, this does not necessarily mean that Vonnegut does not condemn certain actions. Vonnegut's work attempts to show the complexity of human relations and the impossibility of a world painted in simple strokes of black and white.

13. In using the term *devolution* in this context, I am well aware that some may consider the process described as evolutionary. The entire novel works within this paradox and depends upon one's interpretation of the human transformation to a seal-like state. If one deems such a transformation to be a positive step forward, then the process must be described as evolutionary; if, however, one deems the loss of the human brain and all the various abilities that go with the possession of such an organ as a movement backward, then the condition may best be described as devolutionary. As I stated earlier, it appears that Vonnegut is

ambivalent; he certainly values many of the achievements of humanity made possible by our brains—Beethoven's Ninth Symphony, for example—but, at the same time, he remains skeptical of our ability to survive the destruction only our brains make possible.

14. In an interview in 1987, Vonnegut responded facetiously to Allen's comment that the loss of the complexity of human thought would be a tragedy by saying, "I don't see why" (*Conversations* 292). Of course, Vonnegut's actions and words seem to belie any easy acceptance of such a loss. In "Surviving the End: Apocalypse, Evolution, and Entropy in Bernard Malamud, Kurt Vonnegut, and Thomas Pynchon," Peter Freese concludes that *Galápagos*, by existing and being an imaginative tale, "articulates faith in the redemptive power of language and the sense-making ability of story-telling, thereby affirming the distinctive faculties of man that it so ironically purports to get rid of" (171).

15. For a detailed discussion of Vonnegut's use of art history see David Rampton's essay, "Into the Secret Chamber: Art and the Artist in Kurt Vonnegut's *Bluebeard*." Rampton closely examines Vonnegut's considerable knowledge of twentieth-century art and lauds Vonnegut's use of the abstract expressionist movement as a foregrounding device.

16. When I speak of Marilee's maternal nature, I do not mean to downplay the romantic love Rabo feels for Marilee. Marilee's maternal qualities, of course, are only a part of who she is as a complete person. For this reason, we should not overlook the beautiful physicality of their sexual union as described by Rabo. Rabo even says of their sole sexual encounter, "I like to think we were man and wife" (170). But because of the ten-year age difference—Rabo was nineteen and Marilee was twenty-nine—and the difference in their understanding of the world, they remain separated. Unlike Rabo, for the most part Marilee views their relationship more as that of an older sister and brother; she is far more interested in nurturing Rabo than she is in bedding him.

17. As in *Slaughterhouse-Five*, Vonnegut again attacks the depiction of war in the movies. Rabo and another abstract expressionist painter discuss their involvement in the war and loathe the manner it is portrayed on the silver screen:

> "All the returning veterans in the movies are our age or older," he said. That was true. In the movies you seldom saw the babies who had done most of the heavy fighting on the ground in the war.

"Yes—" I said, "and most of the actors in the movies never even went to war. They came home to the wife and kids and swimming pool after every grueling day in front of the cameras, after firing off blank cartridges while men all around them were spitting catsup."

"That's what the young people will think our war was fifty years from now," said Kitchen, "old men and blanks and catsup." So they would. So they do.

"Because of the movies," he predicted, "nobody will believe that it was babies who fought the war." (257)

The role of cinema in shaping the way people think and act represents Vonnegut's larger conception of the force of art. Vonnegut hopes if cinema can transform its viewers, then, perhaps, writing and painting and music can also be used as tools for the social good.

18. Allen points out that Vonnegut's depiction of women has changed dramatically over the course of his career: "It would be fair to call *Bluebeard* a profeminist novel, since women and their struggles in a patriarchal world figure so importantly in it, and because women finally emerge as generally morally superior to men" (*Understanding* 163).

19. Although Eugene continually enters into relationships with married women, he does so more from a desire to touch the lonely and distressed than to use another human being for sexual pleasure alone. Eugene's own wife and her mother have gone insane—a condition that runs in their family—and he faithfully cares for both of their needs. Broer suggests that Eugene's adulterous affairs and his care for his wife and mother-in-law represent Eugene's potential as a "healer of others" (179).

Works Cited

Allen, William Rodney, ed. *Conversations with Kurt Vonnegut*. Jackson: UP of Mississippi, 1988.

———. *Understanding Kurt Vonnegut*. Columbia: U of South Carolina P, 1991.

Antczak, Frederick J. "Teaching Rhetoric and Teaching Morality: Some Problems and Possibilities of Ethical Criticism." *Rhetoric Society Quarterly* 19 (1989): 15–22.

Barthes, Roland. "The World of Wrestling." *Contemporary Critical Theory*. Ed. Dan Latimer. New York: Harcourt Brace Jovanovich, 1989. 45–54.

Baudrillard, Jean. "The Precession of Simulacra." *A Postmodern Reader*. Ed. Joseph Natoli and Linda Hutcheon. Albany: State U of New York P, 1993. 342–75.

———. *The Transparency of Evil*. Trans. James Benedict. New York: Verso, 1993.

Bauman, Zygmunt. "Postmodernity, or Living with Ambivalence." *A Postmodern Reader*. Ed. Joseph Natoli and Linda Hutcheon. Albany: State U of New York P, 1993. 9–24.

Berry, Wendell. *The Unforeseen Wilderness*. San Francisco: North Point Press, 1991.

———. *The Unsettling of America: Culture & Agriculture*. San Francisco: Sierra Club, 1977.

Best, Steven, and Douglas Kellner. *Postmodern Theory: Critical Interrogations*. New York: The Guilford Press, 1991.

Boon, Kevin Alexander. *At Millennium's End: New Essays on the Work of Kurt Vonnegut*. Albany: State U of New York P, 2001.

Booth, Wayne C. *The Company We Keep: An Ethics of Fiction*. Berkeley: U of California P, 1988.

Broer, Lawrence R. *Sanity Plea: Schizophrenia in the Novels of Kurt Vonnegut*. Tuscaloosa: U of Alabama P, 1994.

Buechner, Frederick. *Whistling in the Dark: A Doubter's Dictionary*. San Francisco: HarperCollins, 1988.

Burhans, Clinton S. "Hemingway and Vonnegut: Diminishing Vision in a Dying Age." *Modern Fiction Studies* 21 (1975): 173–91.

Butler, Judith. "Gender Trouble, Feminist Theory, and Psychoanalytic Discourse." *Feminism/Postmodernism*. Ed. Linda J. Nicholson. New York: Routledge, 1990. 324–40.

Clausen, Christopher. *The Moral Imagination: Essays on Literature and Ethics*. Iowa City: U of Iowa P, 1986.

Coles, Robert. "Putting Head and Heart on the Line." *The Chronicle of Higher Education*. 26 October 1994: A64.

Davis, Todd F., and Kenneth Womack. *Mapping the Ethical Turn: A Reader in Ethics, Culture, and Literary Theory*. Charlottesville: U of Virginia P, 2001.

Des Pres, Terrence. *Writing into the World: Essays 1973–1987*. New York: Viking, 1991.

Franklin, Benjamin. *The Autobiography of Benjamin Franklin*. New York: Houghton Mifflin, 1923.

Freese, Peter. "Surviving the End: Apocalypse, Evolution, and Entropy in Bernard Malamud, Kurt Vonnegut, and Thomas Pynchon." *Critique* 36 (1995): 163–76.

Friedman, Bruce J. *Black Humor*. New York: Bantam, 1969.

Fussell, Paul. *The Great War and Modern Memory*. Oxford: Oxford UP, 1975.

———. *Wartime: Understanding and Behavior in the Second World War*. Oxford: Oxford UP, 1989.

Gardner, John. *On Moral Fiction*. New York: Basic Books, 1978.

Giannone, Richard. *Vonnegut: A Preface to His Novels*. Port Washington: Kennikat Press, 1977.

Giroux, Henry. "Postmodernism as Border Pedagogy: Redefining the Boundaries of Race and Ethnicity." *A Postmodern Reader*. Ed. Joseph Natoli and Linda Hutcheon. Albany: State U of New York P, 1993. 452–96.

Godshalk, William L. "Vonnegut and Shakespeare: Rosewater at Elsinore." *The Critical Response to Kurt Vonnegut*. Ed. Leonard Mustazza. Westport: Greenwood P, 1994. 99–106.

Harris, Charles B. "Illusion and Absurdity: The Novels of Kurt Vonnegut." *Critical Essays on Kurt Vonnegut*. Ed. Robert Merrill. Boston: G.K. Hall, 1990. 131–41.

Hassan, Ihab. *Paracriticisms: Seven Speculations of the Times*. Urbana: U of Illinois P, 1975.

———. *The Postmodern Turn: Essays in Postmodern Theory and Culture*. Columbus: Ohio State UP, 1987.

Horne, Haynes. "Jameson's Strategies of Containment." *Postmodernism/ Jameson/ Critique*. Ed. Douglas Kellner. Washington, DC: Maisonneuve P, 1989. 268–300.

Hume, Kathryn. "Kurt Vonnegut and the Myths and Symbols of Meaning." *Texas Studies in Literature and Language* 24:4 (1982): 429–46.

Hutcheon, Linda. "Historiographic Metafiction: Parody and the Intertextuality of History." *Intertextuality and Contemporary American Fiction*. Ed. Patrick O'Donnell and Robert Con Davis. Baltimore: Johns Hopkins UP, 1989. 3–32.

———. *A Poetics of Postmodernism: History, Theory Fiction*. New York: Routledge, 1988.

Irving, John. "Kurt Vonnegut and His Critics." *New Republic* 22 September 1979: 41–49.

———. *The World According to Garp*. New York: Dutton, 1976.

Jameson, Fredric R. "Postmodernism, or The Cultural Logic of Late Capitalism." *New Left Review* 146 (1984): 52–92.

Kellner, Douglas. "Critical Theory vs. Postmodern Theory: Contemporary Debates in Social Theory." Departments of Philosophy, Sociology, & English, Northern Illinois University. DeKalb, 13 October 1994.

———. "Postmodernism as Social Theory: Some Challenges and Problems." *Theory, Culture & Society* 5 (1988): 239–69.

Klinkowitz, Jerome. *Kurt Vonnegut.* London: Methuen, 1982.

———. *Literary Disruptions: The Making of a Post-Contemporary American Fiction.* 2nd ed. Urbana: U of Illinois P, 1980.

———. Rev. of *Slapstick*, by Kurt Vonnegut. *The Critical Response to Kurt Vonnegut.* Ed. Leonard Mustazza. Westport: Greenwood P, 1994. 187–88.

———. *Structuring the Void: The Struggle for Subject in Contemporary American Fiction.* Durham: Duke UP, 1992.

———. *Vonnegut in Fact: The Public Spokesmanship of Personal Fiction.* Columbia, SC: U of South Carolina P, 1998.

Klinkowitz, Jerome, and Donald L. Lawler, eds. *Vonnegut in America: An Introduction to the Life and Work of Kurt Vonnegut.* New York: Delta, 1977.

Klinkowitz, Jerome, and John Somer, eds. *The Vonnegut Statement: Original Essays on the Life and Works of Kurt Vonnegut, Jr.* New York: Delta, 1973.

Lee, Charles. "New Terms and Goons." Rev. of *Player Piano*, by Kurt Vonnegut. *Saturday Review* 30 August 1952: 11.

Leeds, Marc. *The Vonnegut Encyclopedia: An Authorized Compendium.* Westport: Greenwood P, 1994.

Leonard, John. "Black Magic." Rev. of *Hocus Pocus*, by Kurt Vonnegut. *The Critical Response to Kurt Vonnegut.* Ed. Leonard Mustazza. Westport: Greenwood P, 1994. 301–07.

Lodge, David. *Nice Work.* New York: Penguin, 1988.

Lundquist, James. *Kurt Vonnegut.* New York: Ungar, 1977.

Lyotard, Jean-François. *The Differend: Phrases in Dispute.* Trans. George Van Den Abbeele. Minneapolis: University of Minnesota P, 1983.

———. "Interview." *Theory, Culture & Society* 5 (1988): 277–309.

———. *The Postmodern Condition: A Report on Knowledge.* Trans. Geoff Bennington and Brian Massumi. Minneapolis: University of Minnesota P, 1984.

Lyotard, Jean-François, and Jean-Loup Thebaud. *Just Gaming*. Trans. Brian Massumi. Minneapolis: University of Minnesota P, 1985.

May, John R. "Vonnegut's Humor and the Limits of Hope." *The Critical Response to Kurt Vonnegut*. Ed. Leonard Mustazza. Westport: Greenwood P, 1994. 123–33.

McGowan, John. "Postmodernism." *The Johns Hopkins Guide to Literary Theory & Criticism*. Ed. Michael Groden and Martin Kreiswirth. Baltimore: Johns Hopkins UP, 1994. 585–87.

———. *Postmodernism and Its Critics*. Ithaca: Cornell UP, 1991.

McHale, Brian. *Postmodernist Fiction*. London: Methuen, 1987.

McInerney, Jay. "Still Asking the Embarrassing Questions." *New York Times Book Review* 9 September 1990: 12.

Mellard, James M. *The Exploded Form: The Modernist Novel in America*. Urbana: U of Illinois P, 1980.

Merrill, Robert. Introduction. *Critical Essays on Kurt Vonnegut*. Ed. Robert Merrill. Boston: G.K. Hall, 1990. 1–27.

———. "Foreword—Ethics/Aesthetics: A Post-Modern Position." *Ethics/ Aesthetics: Post-Modern Positions*. Washington, DC: Maisonneuve Press, 1988. vii–xiii.

Miller, James B. "The Emerging Postmodern World." *Postmodern Theology: Christian Faith in a Pluralist World*. Ed. Frederic B. Burnham. San Francisco: Harper & Row, 1989. 1–19.

Miller, J. Hillis. *The Ethics of Reading: Kant, de Man, Eliot, Trollope, James, and Benjamin*. New York: Columbia UP, 1987.

———. *Versions of Pygmalion*. Cambridge: Harvard UP, 1990.

Mustazza, Leonard, ed. *The Critical Response to Kurt Vonnegut*. Westport: Greenwood P, 1994.

———. "A Darwinian Eden: Science and Myth in Kurt Vonnegut's *Galápagos*." *The Critical Response to Kurt Vonnegut*. Ed. Leonard Mustazza. Westport: Greenwood P, 1994. 279–86.

———. *Forever Pursuing Genesis: The Myth of Eden in the Novels of Kurt Vonnegut*. Lewisburg: Bucknell UP, 1990.

Nussbaum, Martha C. *Love's Knowledge: Essays on Philosophy and Literature*. Oxford: Oxford UP, 1990.

Olderman, Raymond M. *Beyond the Waste Land: The American Novel in the Nineteen Sixties*. New Haven: Yale UP, 1972.

Parr, Susan Resneck. *The Moral of the Story: Literature, Values, and American Education*. New York: Teachers College Press, 1982.

Pickrel, Paul. "Outstanding Novels." Rev. of *Player Piano*, by Kurt Vonnegut. *The Yale Review* Autumn 1952: 20.

Prescott, Peter S. "Nothing Sacred." *Critical Essays on Kurt Vonnegut*. Ed. Robert Merrill. Boston: G.K. Hall, 1990. 39–40.

Rackstraw, Loree. "Paradise Re-Lost." Rev. of *Slapstick*, by Kurt Vonnegut. *The Critical Response to Kurt Vonnegut*. Ed. Leonard Mustazza. Westport: Greenwood P, 1994. 189–92.

Rampton, David. "Into the Secret Chamber: Art and the Artist in Kurt Vonnegut's *Bluebeard*." *Critique* 35 (1993): 16–26.

———. "The Later Vonnegut." *Vonnegut in America*. Ed. Jerome Klinkowitz and Donald L. Lawler. New York: Delta, 1977. 150–86.

Reed, Peter J., and Marc Leeds. *The Vonnegut Chronicles: Interviews and Essays*. Westport, CT: Greenwood Press, 1996.

Rosenau, Pauline Marie. *Postmodernism and the Social Sciences: Insights, Inroads, and Intrusions*. Princeton: Princeton UP, 1992.

Sale, Roger. Rev. of *Slapstick*. *New York Times Book Review* 3 October 1976: 3.

Schickel, Richard. Rev. of *Mother Night*. *Harper's* May 1966: 103.

Schatt, Stanley. "The Whale and the Cross: Vonnegut's Jonah and Christ Figures." *Southwest Review* 56 (1971): 29–42.

Scholes, Robert. "Chasing a Lone Eagle: Vonnegut's College Writing." *The Vonnegut Statement: Original Essays on the Life and Work of Kurt Vonnegut, Jr.* Ed. Jerome Klinkowitz and John Somer. New York: Delta, 1973. 45–54.

———. "Kurt Vonnegut and Black Humor." *Critical Essays on Kurt Vonnegut*. Ed. Robert Merrill. Boston: G.K. Hall, 1990. 74–82.

Schriber, Mary Sue. "Bringing Chaos to Order: The Novel Tradition and Kurt Vonnegut, Jr." *Genre* 10 (1977): 283–97.

Siebers, Tobin. *The Ethics of Criticism*. Ithaca: Cornell UP, 1988.

Slemon, Stephen. "Modernism's Last Post." *A Postmodern Reader*. Ed. Joseph Natoli and Linda Hutcheon. Albany: State U of New York P, 1993. 426–39.

Snider, Merlin. "Morals and Irreligion: Kurt Vonnegut as Social Ethicist." Diss. University of Southern California, 1988.

Spacks, Patricia Meyer. "The Novel as Ethical Paradigm." *Why the Novel Matters: A Postmodern Perplex*. Ed. Mark Spilka and Caroline McCracken-Flesher. Bloomington: Indiana UP, 1990. 199–205.

Tompkins, Jane P. *Sensational Designs: The Cultural Work of American Fiction, 1790–1860*. New York: Oxford UP, 1985.

Tunnell, James R. "Kesey and Vonnegut: Preachers of Redemption." *A Casebook on Ken Kesey's* One Flew Over the Cuckoo's Nest. Ed. George J. Searles. Albuquerque: U of New Mexico P, 1992. 127–33.

Updike, John. "All's Well in Skyscraper National Park." Rev. of *Slapstick*, by Kurt Vonnegut. *Critical Essays on Kurt Vonnegut*. Ed. Robert Merrill. Boston: G.K. Hall, 1990. 40–47.

Vonnegut, Clemens. *Instruction in Morals*. Indianapolis: Hollenbeck Press, 1990.

Vonnegut, Kurt. *Between Time and Timbuktu or Prometheus–5*. New York: Dell, 1972.

———. *Bluebeard*. New York: Delacorte Press, 1987.

———. *Breakfast of Champions*. New York: Dell, 1973.

———. *Cat's Cradle*. New York: Dell, 1963.

———. *Deadeye Dick*. New York: Delacorte Press/Seymour Lawrence, 1982.

———. *Fates Worse Than Death*. New York: G. P. Putnam, 1991.

———. *Galápagos*. New York: Delacorte Press/Seymour Lawrence, 1985.

———. "General Electric News Bureau News Release, 3 January 1950." *Playboy*. December 1973: 229.

———. *God Bless You, Dr. Kevorkian*. New York: Seven Stories Press, 1999.

———. *God Bless You, Mr. Rosewater*. New York: Dell, 1965.

——. *Happy Birthday, Wanda June.* New York: Dell, 1970.

——. *Hocus Pocus.* New York: G. P. Putnam's Sons, 1990.

——. Interview. *Playboy.* July 1973: 57–60, 62, 66, 68, 70, 72, 74, 214, 216.

——. *JailBird.* New York: Delacorte Press/Seymour Lawrence, 1979.

——. *Mother Night.* New York: Dell, 1966.

——. *Palm Sunday.* New York: Delacorte Press, 1981.

——. *Player Piano.* New York: Dell, 1952.

——. *Sirens of Titan.* New York: Dell, 1959.

——. *Slapstick.* New York: Delacorte Press/Seymour Lawrence, 1976.

——. *Slaughterhouse-Five.* New York: Dell, 1969.

——. *Sun Moon Star.* New York: Harper & Row, 1980.

——. *Timequake.* New York: G. P. Putnam, 1997.

——. *Wampeters, Foma, & Granfalloons.* New York: Dell, 1976.

Vonnegut, Kurt, and Lee Stringer. *Like Shaking Hands with God: A Conversation about Writing.* New York: Seven Stories Press, 1999.

Vonnegut, Mark. *The Eden Express.* New York: Praeger, 1975.

Wiesel, Elie. *From the Kingdom of Memory.* New York: Summit Books, 1990.

Wymer, Thomas. "The Swiftian Satire of Kurt Vonnegut, Jr." *Voices for the Future.* Ed. Thomas D. Clareson. Bowling Green: Bowling Green U Popular P, 1976. 238–62.

Yarbrough, Stephen R. *Deliberate Criticism: Toward a Postmodern Humanism.* Athens: U of Georgia P, 1992.

Yarmolinsky, Jane Vonnegut. *Angels without Wings.* Houghton Mifflin, 1987.

Ziegfeld, Richard. "Kurt Vonnegut on Censorship and Moral Values." *Modern Fiction Studies* 26 (1981): 631–35.

Index